MANCHESTER AT WAR

CLIVE HARDY
IAN COOPER
HENRY HOCHLAND

1

Published by Archive Publications Ltd., 27 York Road, Bowdon, Cheshire WA14 3EF.
Printed & Photoset by Mitchell & Wright (Printers) Ltd., Queen Anne Street, Southport.
ISBN 0 948946 01 6 hbk
ISBN 0 948946 00 8 pbk

2

INTRODUCTION

The idea behind this book is to present a photographic account of life in wartime Manchester, Salford and the surrounding areas. It is not a definitive work on the subject, space does not allow for it, but what we hope we have achieved is to recapture something of the spirit of 40 years ago.

The Second World War directly affected the lives of every man, woman and child in this country. From evacuation to Air Raid Precautions, from rationing to being directed where one could or could not work, to service with the Armed Forces or the Home Guard; there was no escape.

The photographs for this volume have been drawn together from a wide variety of sources and from as far afield as Southampton, Birmingham, London, Sheffield and Wolverhampton. Local sources are too numerous to mention here, but we trust that we have acknowledged, in the appropriate section at the back of the book, all those who have assisted in its preparation.

Regrettably, a number of photographs have had to be omitted from this volume. However, a second volume is planned which will include some of the material we were unable to use in this book together with any interesting material you, the reader, may have. We would be delighted to receive any wartime photographs and stories for possible inclusion in Volume 2 - all the details are on Page 112 - Can you help?

February 1986.

Clive Hardy
Ian Cooper
Henry Hochland

CONTENTS

THE ROAD TO WAR

In May 1937 following Stanley Baldwin's resignation, Neville Chamberlain was appointed Prime Minister. Chamberlain was nearly seventy years old, had a lean hawkish look about him and always dressed in forbidding dark clothes and wing collars.

As Prime Minister, he proved to be obstinate, impatient of criticism and secretive. He could be a natural dictator, ruling over his Cabinet with a rod of iron and was blessed with an undemocratic arrogance to the point of ignoring parliament and evading debate. On top of all this, Chamberlain distrusted officials at the Foreign Office and would not hesitate in circumventing them in order to pursue his brand of personal diplomacy. In matters of Foreign Policy, Chamberlain had no love for the Soviet Union and his dealings with France, though inescapable, proved to be far from cordial. Above all else, his hatred of war was without doubt both passionate and sincere. He followed what he himself called a "general scheme of appeasement" in the belief that it would solve Europe's problems and save us from ever again having to experience the horror and slaughter of the Great War. But by 1937 the world was already heading inexorably towards an even greater and bloodier confrontation.

The Treaty of Versailles had placed the responsibility for the outbreak of the First World War upon Germany and her Allies. Under the terms of the treaty, Germany was virtually disarmed and relieved of her overseas possessions. The provinces of Alsace-Lorraine were ceded to France, Eupen and Malmedy went to Belgium and Poland was given to West Prussia and Posen. Memel, Danzig and the Saar were placed under military occupation and no German troops were to be stationed within fifty miles of the east bank of the Rhine. In 1921, it was finally decided that Germany should pay her former enemies reparations to the value of 136,000 million gold marks, a figure far beyond her means. Of the treaty Marshal Foch said "This is not peace, it is an armistice for twenty years."

Of Germany's former allies, the once almighty Austria-Hungarian Empire had collapsed into anarchy towards the end of the war. The central Hapsburg Government which had for so long held together in uneasy companionship Serbs, Magyars, Austrians, Slovaks and a score of other races and ethnic minorities ceased to function. The result was that the empire split into a number of successor states who began to squabble amongst themselves over the position of new frontiers.

It was hoped that the external politics of states would in future be settled by a new organisation, the League of Nations. The League had been set up specifically to promote international peace through collective security. Unhappily the League failed. On a number of occasions the assembly dithered and any pretences of a collective security system were shredded in September 1931 when Japan invaded with impunity China's northern most province Manchuria.

In December 1934, a frontier dispute as Wal Wal was used by the Italians as a pretext to make 'defensive' preparations and pour troops, tanks and artillery into Italian Somaliland. For ten months, Abyssinia appealed to the League to arbitrate. On the 3rd October the Italians invaded. In November economic and financial sanctions were half-heartedly imposed on Italy. A month later, Foreign Secretary Sir Samuel Hoare and his French opposite number Pierre Laval concocted a plan whereby two-thirds of Abyssinia would be handed over to the Italians in the name of peace. The Times, though usually an open supporter of appeasement, denounced the proposals, and Bawldwin, albeit temporarily, sacked Hoare to save his own political neck. At the end of April 1936, Haile Selassie made his final appeal to the League for help. "I must still hold on until my tardy allies appear, and if they never come then I say prophetically and without bitterness, the West will perish." A week later, Italian troops entered Addis Ababa, Haile Selassie fled into exile and Italy formally announced the annexation of Abbyssinia.

In October 1929, a brand new luxury apartment on New York's plush Fifth Avenue cost around 1500 dollars a week to rent and tickets to a Broadway theatre averaged 28 dollars each. By the end of November, the Fifth Avenue rental had been slashed to 150 dollars and the theatre tickets were down in price to 2-3 dollars each. The financial crisis at the New York Stock Exchange, Wall Street, had started to bite. American industry had grown rapidly since the end of the Great War due to a deliberate policy of readily available loans by the Federal Reserve Bank. In Europe, United States loans between 1925-1929 amounted to a staggering 2,900 million dollars, and though some countries, including Britain, were suffering from overseas competition for their traditional industries, others, inlcuding Czechoslovakia, Austria and Germany were enjoying a period of relative prosperity. In July 1929, the supply of goods in the United States finally outstripped demand, necessitating a reduction in output and reduncancies. Investors began to lose confidence and substantial losses on share prices occured. By the end of October, 18,000 million dollars had been wiped off the value of shares. The Wall Street Crash however had only just begun, for though a modest recovery was made during the first months of 1930, in June, the market began another slide that lasted unabated for twenty-five months. By July 1932, the value of all stocks listed on Wall Street shrank from 90,000 million dollars to under 16,000 million and the effect was worldwide.

In 1931, Europe was rocked by a banking crisis with the collapse of the Vienna Bank in Austria and a run on the Reichsbank in Germany. Severe financial strain was placed on London and the Labour Government, which was already battling against the slump and a dole queue of 2 million was unable to put together a programme of economy measures. The Government resigned and Ramsey MaDonald together with a handful of labour M.P.'s joined forces with the Conservatives to form a 'National' Government. One of Labour's more able members, Sir Oswald Moseley, Chancellor of the Duchy of Lancaster, had already left the government because the Cabinet had failed to agree to his scheme for bringing down unemployment with a programme of public works, a higher school leaving age, early retirement and the control of credit through the banks. Moseley and his followers formed the New Party which eventually became the British Union of Fascists.

At the height of the depression nearly three million insured workers were without jobs and this figure did not include the self-employed, agricultural workers and women who either did not, or were not, eligable for registration. In the south-east, one worker in nine was on the dole. In Tyneside, Lancashire, South Wales and Clydeside, where a reliance of work had rested with the traditional industries, unemployment was at one in three or four of the workforce. In the Bishop Auckland area of Durham, there had been 33 pits employing 28,000 miners. By 1935 only thirteen pits were still in production employing 6,500 men on a part-time basis. In 1934, 67.8 per cent of insured workers in Jarrow were on the dole. In Gateshead the figure was 44.23 per cent and in Merthyr it was 61.9 per cent. On the other hand in High Wycombe, unemployment stood at 3.3 per cent of insured workers and in St. Albans the figure was 3.9 per cent. Without doubt the misery caused by unemployment could, and was, ignored by the well off.

It was in an attempt to publicise their plight that the National Unemployed Worker's Movement (N.U.W.M.) organised a series of marches and demonstrations throughout the country. On the 1st October 1931, several hundred demonstrators gathered in the square in front of Salford Town Hall to protest at cuts in unemployment benefit. In a pitched battle with police, twelve demonstrators were arrested. The following day, some 2,000 men turned up to protest against the arrests. A week later 5,000 assembled at Ardwick Green, their intention being to walk to Manchester Town Hall and present a petition. When police informed the marchers that they could not follow their intended route into the city fighting broke out. Thirty-eight arrests were made and six men were injured. The next day, fearing further trouble, the police mounted guard on public buildings, banks and shops in the Salford and Manchester area and there was a mobilisation of Special Constables on a scale not seen since the darkest days of the General Strike. The N.U.W.M. continued its campaign into 1932. The worst disturbances occured in Belfast where police were forced to open fire on demonstrators in self defence.

Due to the economy cuts, between 1931-35, an unemployed man with a wife and three children to support could expect to receive 29/3d a week benefit or as 'transitional payments' once benefit had been exhausted. Transitional payments were subject to means testing, a particularly viscous piece of legislation in which earnings, savings, pensions and other assets of a family were taken into account before an award was made. It was automatically assumed that the assets were available to support an unemployed man. Children, if they lived at home, were forced to support out of work parents and the authorities encouraged neighbours to spy and inform on one another. Large numbers were cut off from benefit by the means test and in Lancashire, it has been claimed that a third of all applicants were refused help.

In 1932, it was estimated that at least 89,000 people were living two or more to a room in Liverpool. In Birmingham the figure was put at 68,000 and in Manchester around 49,000 people lived in overcrowded conditions. Sir Ernest Simon once described the conditions he found in one house in the slum district of Angel Meadow.

> "The general appearance and conditon of this house inside is very miserable. It is dark and the plaster on the passage walls, in particular, was in a bad condition. There is no sink or tap in the house; they are in a small yard, consequently in frosty weather the family is without water. In the house live a man and wife, seven children, ranging in age from 15 to 1, and a very large, if varying, number of rats."

Manchester did have plans to demolish its slums. The old Wythenshawe estate had been bought by the city and Sir Ernest planned to house 100,000 people on the 2,500 acre estate. By 1939, 7,000 new houses had been built at Wythenshawe and plans were afoot for a large-scale reconstruction of the southern half of the city.

It was not until Sir Malcolm Stewart's ideas were accepted in the Special Areas (Amendment) Act, 1937, that the possibilities for creating any large-scale employment occurred. Sir Malcom's proposal was that in return for opening a factory in a depressed area, a firm should be offered tax, rent and rates incentives for a period of five years. Sir Malcolm's vision led to the opening of a number of trading estates, where firms could lease premises with all services laid on. Initially the trading estates attracted only light industries, but by the end of 1937 unemployment figures for the Special Areas had fallen by 155,000 though 67,000 of these were due to people moving away. By 1937 rearmament was beginning to take up spare capacity in industry and new jobs were being created.

THE RISE OF THE NAZIS

In Germany in 1932 unemployment stood at 6 million and was still rising. It was out of the misery of unemployment and low pay for those fortunate enough to be in work, that the class, ideological and racial doctrines of the National Socialist Party (Nazis) grew and prospered in the Weimar Republic. In July 1932, the Nazis' polled 37.3 per cent of the vote, which under the republic's system of proportional representation gave them 230 seats in the Reichstag. The Nazis were now the largest single party in parliament, and despite his known dislike for their politics, aging President Hindenberg had little alternative but to summon the Nazis leader, Adolf Hitler, to the Chancellorship in January 1933.

Hitler was a charismatic figure and a political opportunist, but he was totally committed in his desire to see Germany once more established as the leading European power.

Hitler's first priority was to make his own position and authority unassailable. On the 28th February, a decree was issued under Article 48 of the Constitution suspending normal civil liberties. In March came the 'Communist' plot culminating in the burning down of the Reichstag. Using article 48, Hitler expelled the 83 Communist members of parliament and by reaching an accord with the Centre Party acheived the necessary majority required to pass the Enabling Law which empowered the Chancellor to issue legislation without having to seek the consent of parliament.

From 1934 onwards, Hitler was to push rearmament and the reinflation of the German economy as far as he could. It was not a straight-forward task. Germany lacked foreign exchange which hampered imports, especially iron ore and the only raw material that she had in relative abundance was coal. On the 9th March 1935, Germany for the first time officially acknowledged the existance of her Air Force (Luftwaffe). A week later, conscription was introduced, the peace-time strength of the Army being set at 550,000 men. By the end of the year the German Navy had launched no less than nineteen submarines, though these were coastal types for training, rather than for front-line use.

In 1936, Hitler played one of his political hunches and ordered the re-occupation of the Rhineland. Britain and France failed to act.

ANSCHLUSS & CZECHOSLOVAKIA

Hitler had long dreamed of incorporating his native Austria into the reich and by the beginning of 1938 he was ready to move.

On the 19th November 1937, Lord Halifax had visited Hitler in Bavaria, to discuss the possibility of Germany obtaining colonies in Africa - at the expense of Portugal and Belgium, though neither country had been consulted - in return for arms limitations. Hitler, not surprisingly, was totally unimpressed. He was not interested in overseas colonies, which could easily be cut off in time of war. The empire he wished to create was in Europe. Austria would be the first aquisition before his push along the ancient Teutonic path towards the east.

On the 12th February, he invited the Austrian Chancellor, Kurt von Schuschnigg, to Berchtesgaden. The route Schuschnigg's car took was lined somewhat menacingly with troops of the 120,000 strong Austrian Legion. By the end of the meeting Schuschnigg had been pressured into agreeing to include Austrian Nazis in his cabinet. The question of unification (Anschluss) was raised but no formal agreement was reached. Hitler got the shock of his life a couple of weeks later when Schuschnigg announced that the question of Anschluss would have to be decided by plebiscite. Fearing that the vote could go against unification, the German High Command improvised invasion plans during the night of 9th/10th March. Austria was annexed on the 12th March and on the following day Adolf Hitler paraded in triumph through the streets of Vienna. Once again Britain and France dithered and did nothing.

Neville Chamberlain's idea of purchasing peace through appeasement was that any settlement should involve concessions on both sides, which would thereafter be honoured. Czechoslovakia was another matter.

On the 20th February 1938, Hitler gave a speech in which he promised protection for all Germans living outside the Reich. The speech was siezed upon by the Sudeten Nazis in Czechoslovakia to intensify their campaign for self-determination.

On the 28th/29th April, the first of a series of Anglo-French conversations on German intentions and demands in Czechoslovakia took place. British policy towards the Czechs was ill-informed and unsympathetic. Czechoslovakia was not seen as a bastion to be defended but a "last chance for Anglo-German understanding." The French on the other hand were bound by treaty to aid the Czechs if they were attacked. However, the French feared that in the event of war they would be without British support. Outwardly the Anglo-French meetings were shown as the working out of a joint policy. Behind the scenes however, both governments had decided to abandon the Czechs, but a public announcement to that effect in London and Paris would have been political suicide. At all costs French honour had to be seen to be preserved.

During May, the Sudeten Nazis' leader, Konrad Henlein visited London and he reported to Berlin that the British Government was sympathetic to the Sudeten cause. In any case Chamberlain saw no benefit to Britian in an independent Czechoslovakia. Indeed he shared Hitler's dislike of the Czech alliances with France and Russia, though he was influenced by the fact that the Dominions had little sympathy for a British guarantee.

On the 20th May, two days before the Czech Municipal elections, Hitler ordered General Keital to dust off the plans for a pre-emptive strike against the Czechs whilst holding a defensive line in the west against possible French intervention. Hitler believed that any military action against the Czechs had to take place quickly so that Britain and France would not have time to react. Within days, Europe was gripped with the news that German troops were massing along the Czech border. With 35 divisions and tanks far superior to anything in the German Army, the Czechs would certainly have given a good account of themselves.

On the other hand, the German Army had expanded so rapidly that many units were untrained. There was a serious shortage of officers, only six weeks supply of munitions and fuel reserves were only 25 per cent of mobilization requirements. In the air, the Luftwaffe was in a transition phase and with new types of aircraft being introduced. The operational status for the bomber force was only 49 per cent. The fighter arm had 70 per cent of its aircraft at operational status and to add to these problems, 40 per cent of aircrew were not fully trained, also, the reserves of some aircraft lubricants stood at only 6 per cent of the mobilization requirement. The Luftwaffe was in no fit state to get involved in a war of attrition. The German ace was her propaganda machine. Throughout the summer, a superbly conducted campaign gave the impression that Germany's military capability was far greater than it actually was. The Czechs would not act without the promise of French, British or Russian assistance.

On the 4th September, the Czech Government's nerve finally cracked. Fearing civil war, President Benes agreed to all Sudenten demands. On the 13th September, Hitler demanded self-determination for the Sudetenland. The following day rioting broke out and Martial Law was declared. Henlein fled to Berlin. British attempts to deter the Germans from taking action consisted of diplomatic moves pointing to the probability of intervention, while at the same time positively discouraging the Czechs from fighting by hinting at its improbability. Hitler then demanded the annexation of the Sudetenland and the situation became potentially explosive. Chamberlain offered to go to Germany and meet with Hitler in one last effort to find a peaceful solution.

With the French abdicating all initiatives to Britain and Premier Daladier begging Chamberlain to do something, anything, to aviod France having to honour her treaty obligations, Chamberlain flew to Berchtesgaden.

During their three hour talk, Hitler made it plain that unless Britain accepted Germany's claims there was little point in continuing the conversation. Chamberlain was in no position to negotiate an on the spot agreement, however he offered to consult his Cabinet if Germany in the meantime refrained from opening hostilities. Hitler agreed. Chamberlain was convinced that only the cession of the Sudetenland would halt a German invasion. Three days later, Daladier came to London and agreed a plan that would hand over to Germany all areas in Czechoslovakia containing a majority German population. The Czechs found the proposals unacceptable but were left in no doubt whatsoever that Britain would not fight and that France would ignore her treaty obligations.

On the 22nd, Chamberlain was in Godesberg. Sensing victory, Hitler upped the price of peace. He insisted that Czech forces evacuate the German areas but that their military installations must be left intact and a plebiscite be held in all other areas with a German minority. Chamberlain was well aware that British public opinion was hardening against further concessions to Germany and on returning to London held a series of crisis meetings with the Cabinet and later the French. Lord Halifax urged Chamberlain to make one last effort to reach an agreement with the Führer.

The outcome was that Sir Horace Wilson was to deliver to Hitler a personal letter appealling to him to allow the details of any settlement to be overseen by an international committee of Czech, German and British officals. If Hitler refused, Wilson was to tell him that France would stand by the Czechs and that Britain would stand by France.

On the morning of the 26th, British and French officals discussed the military implications of the crisis and war was considered to be a viable option. Later, Chamberlain informed his Cabinet that Britain would support France in the event of war. Hitler had lost his chance to launch a lightening strike. A conference was hurriedly arranged.

On the 29th September, the Munich Conference was convened, though neither Czechoslovakia or the Soviet Union were represented. In reality the conference was little more than a ceremony, though Hitler was persuaded to agree to a progressive occupation of the Sudetenland and a commission to determine which of the remaining areas with a predominantly German character would be occupied by German troops.

On the morning of the 30th, Chamberlain and Hitler signed - upon the initiative of the former - a declaration that the two countries would in future settle any sources of difference by negotiation.

The result of Munich was that Hitler had gained everything he had wanted and at the same time had destroyed France's military credibility, isolated Russia and Poland, and inflicted a diplomatic defeat upon Great Britain.

Chamberlain, had however, averted war. He came home to a hero's welcome. The British press applauded Chamberlain's work but already there was voiced concern over the future. The **Manchester Guardian** said that Czechoslovakia helpless would result in Hitler being able to advance whenever he was ready. The pro-Labour **Reynold's News** exhorted that Chamberlain has destroyed the collective security system; peace had been sacrificed for a semblance of peace.

POLAND

On the 24th March 1939, Britain and France agreed to resist any German agression against Belgium, Holland and Switzerland. A week later, Britain said she would stand by France in guaranteeing Poland's frontiers. On the 3rd and 11th April, Hitler issued orders for the Wehrmacht to prepare for an invasion of Poland.

With a population of 27 million, Poland's affairs were dominated by her relations with her neighbours, none of whom were to pleased with the frontiers settled on her by the treaty of Versailles. By the end of 1921, the infant Republic had fought no less than six wars and had heavily defeated the Russians at Komarow. But Poland was bitter. She had been left to fight the Soviet Union alone despite the existence of mutual aid treaties with Britain and France.

On the 25th January 1932, Poland signed a Treaty of Non-aggression with Russia and on the 26th January 1934, a similar ten-year pact was concluded with Nazi Germany.

3

Neville Chamberlain returns from Munich.
"Peace for our time."

The real threat to Poland came after the Nazi Party had gained control of Danzig. There is plenty of evidence to suggest that the Poles seriously considered launching a preventive war against Germany but the western powers refused to get involved. Hitler, inspired by the fact that Britain and France had done nothing to stop him in Austria and Czechoslovakia, decided that the time had come to settle the Danzig question once and for all. The Führer demanded the return of Danzig to the Reich and road and rail links across the Polish Corridor. In return, Hitler offered to guarantee Poland's frontiers. The Poles rejected the demands out of hand.

On the 20th August, the world was stunned by the news that the Soviet Union and Nazi Germany had signed a trade agreement. The same day Hitler demanded annexation of Danzig. Three days later, Russia and Germany signed a non-agression pact undertaking not to attack each other. They also concluded a secret agreement to divide Poland and the Baltic States between them.

On the 24th August, Britain requested American help in Warsaw. US ambassador Kennedy's hysterical reporting of the situation gave the impression in Washington that Chamberlain was forcing the Poles into unilateral concessions with Germany. In fact, what Chamberlain wanted was that the Poles state their willingness to negotiate in order to put Hitler clearly in the wrong should he attack. Also, if Hitler agreed to negotiate, then with luck the Poles would be able to drag out the talks until the winter rains made invasion impossible.

Dawn on the 26th had been the time set by Hitler for the invasion of Poland to begin but on the evening of the 25th the orders were cancelled when Mussolini informed Berlin that Italy was in no position to honour the Axis Treaty without massive military aid. On the 25th, the Führer met with Sir Neville Henderson, British ambassador to Berlin, and informed him that he desired a settlement with Britain. He was prepared to guarantee the British Empire and would approach London with an 'offer' once the Polish question had been settled.

Between the 26-28th August, a series of Cabinet meetings were held to consider the implications of Hitler's message. The British warned Hitler against resorting to force and that Britain would stand by Poland. On the evening of the 28th, Hitler took up the diplomatic initiative by asking Henderson "whether England would be willing to accept an alliance with Germany." The ambassador exceeded his instructions and replied that "speaking personally" he did not exclude such a possibility provided that "the development of events justified it." The Führer's moderate tone raised hopes in London. It was interpreted that he was weakening in his resolve because of Germany's isolated position, and that if brought to the negotiating table he would give in. However, Henderson's response to offers of an Anglo-German military alliance were considered political dynamite which, if leaked, would wreck Anglo-American relations. Henderson was warned against making such personal statements in the future.

On the evening of the 29th, Hitler announced that he would negotiate providing a Polish emissary arrived in Berlin by noon the following day. He denied that this was an ultimatum, though he still hoped to divide Warsaw and London. He was convinced that if Chamberlain could be tempted into an Anglo-German alliance, then two possibilities might arise. Firstly, the Poles might refuse to talk in which case the British would be justified in revoking their treaty obligations. Secondly, if a Polish emissary did arrive and talks broke down, then Chamberlain might refuse to fight on the grounds that the Poles provoked a war. Chamberlain to his credit had no intention whatsoever of being drawn into such a trap and informed his Cabinet that the demand for a Polish emissary was unacceptable and that any Anglo-German aggreement depended upon a just settlement for Poland backed by international guarantees.

At 4pm on the 31st, Hitler decided that he could wait no longer and ordered the invasion to take place at dawn the following morning.

At 4.40am, the German battleship **Schleswig-Holstein** moored in Danzig on a friendship visit opened fire on the Polish fortifications at Westerplatte. An hour later, German troops crossed the Polish frontier, the first serious fighting taking place at Gross-Klonia. The Luftwaffe launched a series of air-strikes against Warsaw, Lódź, Czestochowa, Cracow and Poznán. With only 159 fighter aircraft to defend the entire Polish air space, the PAF resorted to head-on attacks that shredded the nerves of the German bomber pilots, forcing them to break formation and shed their loads wide of their intended targets. Obliged to challenge as many Luftwaffe incursions as possible, the PAF lost irreplaceable men and machines until its strength was whittled away.

The Polish Army, some 40 divisions strong, was overwhelmed in many sectors before reserves could be mobilized. In fact French delays at making a statement of intent had induced the Poles to delay mobilization with the result that 25 per cent of her army never made it to the battlefield.

At this late stage, Britain and France using Mussolini as an intermediary, said that they were willing to negotiate if German troops were withdrawn. Hitler, anticipating a short, sharp war of no more than two weeks duration, rejected the proposals. That afternoon Britain ordered general mobilization and under the Defence Regulations the 'blackout' came into force at sunset.

On the 2nd September, Denmark, Finland, Iceland, Norway, Sweden, Latvia, and Estonia declared their neutrality. Japan stated that she would not support Germany because of the non-aggression pact that the latter had signed with Russia.

That night the British ministers Hore-Belisha, Anderson, de la Warr, Colville, Dorman-Smith, Stanley, Wallace and Elliott met in Sir John Simon's room at the House of Commons. Later, Sir John went to see Chamberlain and told him that the Cabinet believed that war must be declared at once. The Cabinet met in emergency session at 11pm. An Anglo-French ultimatum was delivered to Berlin at 9am the following morning. It expired two hours later without a German reply. We were at war.

4th SEPTEMBER, 1939

GOLD MUST BE SOLD TO THE TREASURY

If you have any gold coins you must take it to the ›ank and sell it to the Treasury. Luxury imports, in-luding motor-cars, clothing and perfumery, are ›anned.

These regulations were issued last night.

Residents in Britain must offer foreign securities and bullion, as well as gold coin, to their bankers.

Foreign exchange to be offered for sale includes currencies ›amed by the Treasury from time to time. Those already named ›nclude:—

U.S. dollars, Guilders, Canadian dollars, ›rgentine pesos, Belgas, Swedish crowns, ›wiss francs, Norwegian crowns and ›rench francs.

Persons may apply through their bankers for ›ermission to retain gold and foreign exchange ›equired to meet contracts, made before the ›oming into force of these regulations, which ›rovide for payments in gold or foreign ex-›hange, for meeting the reasonable require-›ents of trade or business, or for reasonable ›avelling or other personal expenses.

Prices to be paid for gold and foreign ex-›hange offered for sale are to be determined ›y the Treasury, and may be ascertained by in-›uiry at any bank.

The public should continue to transact busi-›ess in foreign exchange and gold through the ›gency of their bankers.

Applications for exchange must be made on ›e appropriate form, and satisfactory evidence ›regard to the transaction proposed must be ›roduced in all cases.

Export of banknotes, gold, securities or ›reign currency is prohibited except with per-›ission.

Traders Must Insure

The order issued by the Board of Trade bans ›e imports, except under licence, of luxuries ›nd goods of which there are sufficient home ›upplies

This will conserve exchange for the addi-›onal purchases of other products required in ›ar time.

The main categories of goods covered by the ›rder are pottery and glass, cutlery, clocks ›nd watches, textile goods and apparel (includ-›g footwear), certain chemicals and paints, ›ap, office machinery (including typewriters), ›otor-cars, musical instruments, perfumery ›nd toilet requisites, toys and games and ›xury foodstuffs.

Traders in Britain who sell goods liable to ›ing's enemy risks must insure them under the ›ar Risks Insurance Act.

This is part of a scheme which the Board of ›rade has put into operation.

Liability of the Board as insurers will be de-›rmined by a policy of insurance issued in a ›rm prescribed in the schedule of the War ›isks (Commodity Insurance) (No. 1) Order.

Insurance is compulsory except where the ›alue of a person's insurable goods does not ex-›ed £1,000.

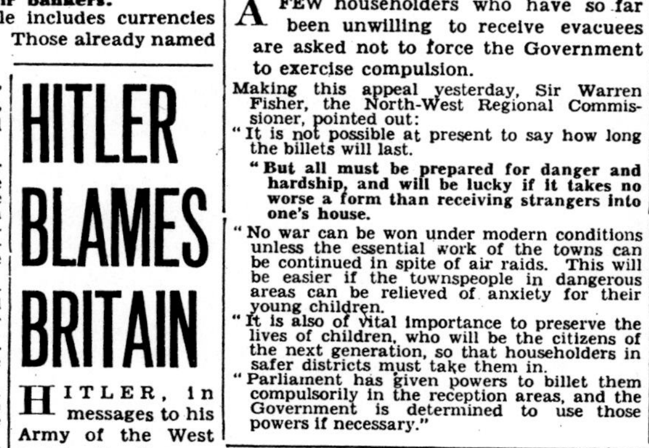

BILLETS BY ORDER, IF—

A FEW householders who have so far been unwilling to receive evacuees are asked not to force the Government to exercise compulsion.

Making this appeal yesterday, Sir Warren Fisher, the North-West Regional Commissioner, pointed out:

"It is not possible at present to say how long the billets will last.

"But all must be prepared for danger and hardship, and will be lucky if it takes no worse a form than receiving strangers into one's house.

"No war can be won under modern conditions unless the essential work of the towns can be continued in spite of air raids. This will be easier if the townspeople in dangerous areas can be relieved of anxiety for their young children.

"It is also of vital importance to preserve the lives of children, who will be the citizens of the next generation, so that householders in safer districts must take them in.

"Parliament has given powers to billet them compulsorily in the reception areas, and the Government is determined to use those powers if necessary."

HITLER BLAMES BRITAIN

HITLER, in messages to his Army of the West and to the German people yesterday, blamed Britain for the war.

He claimed that the Poles had "attacked" Germany, and that he was fighting to "establish peace." He added that he was on the way to the Eastern Front.

To his troops on the Western Front he said (according to the German News Agency, quoted by Reuter):—

"The British Government, driven on by those warmongers whom we knew in the last war, has resolved to let fall its mask and to proclaim war on a threadbare pretext.

"For months it (the British Government) has supported the Polish attacks against the lives and security of fellow-Germans and the rape of the Free City of Danzig," continued Hitler.

"In a Few Months"

"Now that Poland, with the consciousness of this protection, has undertaken acts of aggression against Reich territory, I have determined to blow up this ring which has been laid round Germany.

"Sections of the German Army in the East have now, for two days, in response to Polish attacks, been fighting for the establishment of a peace which shall assure life and freedom to the German people.

"If you do your duty, the battle in the East will have reached its successful conclusion in a few months, and then the power of the whole Nazi State stands behind you.

"As an old soldier of the world war, and as your supreme commander, I am going, with confidence in you, to the Army on the East."

"Unity or—" Threat

To the German people Hitler said the English "encirclement" policy was resumed when the "peaceful" revision of the Versailles Treaty seemed to be succeeding.

To this he added: "The same lying inciters appeared as in 1914."

Claiming that "as long as the German people was united it has never been conquered," Hitler uttered this threat:—

"Whoever offends against this unity need expect nothing else than annihilation as an enemy of the nation."

DUKE TAKES UP NAVAL POST

The Admiralty announces that Rear-Admiral His Royal Highness the Duke of Kent has taken up his war appointment.

Cinemas, Theatres Close to Cut Risks

Immediately after Mr. Chamberlain's dramatic broadcast to the nation, the Government yesterday announced a number of precautionary measures to prevent people crowding together and so increasing the casualty risks from air raids.

Instructions were given for the closing of all places of entertainment until further notice. In the light of experience it may be possible to open cinemas and theatres in some areas later. Included in the closure orders are indoor and outdoor sports gatherings where large numbers of people might be expected to congregate.

The following advice is given:—

Keep off the streets as much as possible; to expose yourself unnecessarily adds to your danger.

Carry your gas mask with you always.

Make sure every member of your household have on them their names and addresses clearly written. Do this on an envelope or luggage label and not on an odd piece of paper which may be lost.

Sew a label on children's clothing so that they cannot pull it off.

People are requested not to crowd together unnecessarily in any circumstances.

Churches and other places of public worship will not be closed.

All day schools in evacuation and neutral areas in England, Wales and Scotland are to be closed for lessons for at least a week from yesterday.

In the reception areas schools will be opened as soon as evacuation is complete.

PETROL IS RATIONED

PETROL rationing will be introduced as from September 16.

This was announced last night by the Secretary for Mines. Information as to how the public can secure their ration books will be announced to-day.

There are very substantial stocks of petrol in the country, but in the national interests the best use must be made of these supplies.

Petrol distributors have arranged to pool all their resources and, after the individual brands still in stock at garages and service stations have been sold by them at prices now ruling, one grade only of motor spirit will be supplied to the public.

This spirit will be called "Pool" motor spirit, and will be on sale, ex-pump, in England and Wales at 1s. 6d. a gallon.

Appeal to Owners

No change will be made in the price for the next fourteen days at least. From to-day no further supplies of individual brands will be made at garages and service stations.

For at least the same period of fourteen days there will be no change in yesterday's bulk prices to those commercial concerns who receive their supplies direct.

Owners and drivers of commercial vehicles are particularly asked to note that it will no longer be possibly to allow commercial vehicles to call at petral companies' depots for supplies.

The Government appeal to all owners of motor vehicles to use them only for essential purposes.

BANKS ARE SHUT TO-DAY

TO-DAY has been declared a limited Bank Holiday, affecting only banks. The arrangement applies to the Post Office Savings Bank and other savings banks.

This day will be used by the banks to complete their measures for adapting themselves to the emergency, and to-morrow morning the banks will be open for business.

The Treasury, in conjunction with the Bank of England, have taken all the steps needed to ensure that the banks (including the Post Office Savings Bank and other savings banks) will be amply supplied with currency.

Postal orders will be legal tender for the present, and Scottish and Northern Ireland banknotes will be legal tender in Scotland and Northern Ireland respectively.

AIR MAIL CURTAILED

Empire air mail-services are from to-day restricted to two services weekly in each direction between the United Kingdom and Sydney and one weekly in each direction between the United Kingdom and Durban and between the United Kingdom and Kisumu.

Corresponding modifications will be made in the overseas connecting services operated by Imperial Airways.

Present arrangements under which first-class mail to certain countries is forwarded by Empire Air Mail services without surcharge will be suspended, and a surcharge will be imposed on all mail from the United Kingdom carried by air on the Empire routes.

Day-old Babies Leave

Three babies born only the previous day were among three trainloads of evacuees from London yesterday.

Accompanied by their mothers, they were driven in an ambulance from the station to a nursing home which has been taken over as a maternity home.

U.S. REFUGEES LEAVE LONDON

BETWEEN two and three thousand American refugees left London last night.

Many of them were destitute.

An American Embassy official said it might take ten days before sufficient ships to evacuate these people will have put in.

Mr. Joseph Kennedy, American Ambassador, has requested all American and other neutral steamship lines to provide all available ships, including freighters and tankers, for evacuation.

WARNINGS TO SHIPPING

The Board of Trade announces: "Shipping is hereby warned that all traffic proceeding through the Dover Straits must proceed through the Downs. Ships disregarding this warning do so at their own peril."

The Admiralty give notice that vessels entering the Firth of Forth must pass to the northward of Bass Rock. Vessels proceeding to the southward of Bass Rock will do so at their own peril.

EVACUATION

Before the outbreak of war, the Government had put forward schemes for the evacuation of schoolchildren and others from those areas thought most likely to be bombed. As the international situation deteriorated, many local authorities organised evacuation rehearsals but on 31st August 1939, special messengers advised the schools that the real thing would take place on the next day, a Friday. The evacuations were spread over three days, Manchester's original estimate being that 80,000 children would leave the city. Special trains were laid on and Manchester Corporation took 140 buses out of scheduled services to help.

On the second day, the main emphasis was on getting mothers with young children under five years of age, expectant mothers and the handicapped evacuated. Some schools were involved, the boys of Manchester Grammar going from Victoria and the girls of Manchester High leaving from London Road Station.

On Sunday, among the schools evacuated were the Central High School for Boys, Chorlton High School and Levenshulme High. There were eighteen special trains carrying mothers with young children. So successful were Manchester's evacuation plans, that when war was declared at eleven o'clock, only nine trains remained to be despatched. In all, 72,000 children and 23,000 adults had been evacuated.

Over 1½ million people were evacuated from towns and cities including 827,000 children, 524,000 mothers and young children, 13,000 expectant mothers, 7,000 handicapped and 103,000 teachers and helpers. There was not one serious or fatal accident.

6

5

Trafford Road School.

Salford children wait at Ordsall Lane Station.

Leaving home: with an identification label round their necks, a gas mask in a cardboard box and a few personal belongings, children assemble at Trafford Road School. 1st September, 1939

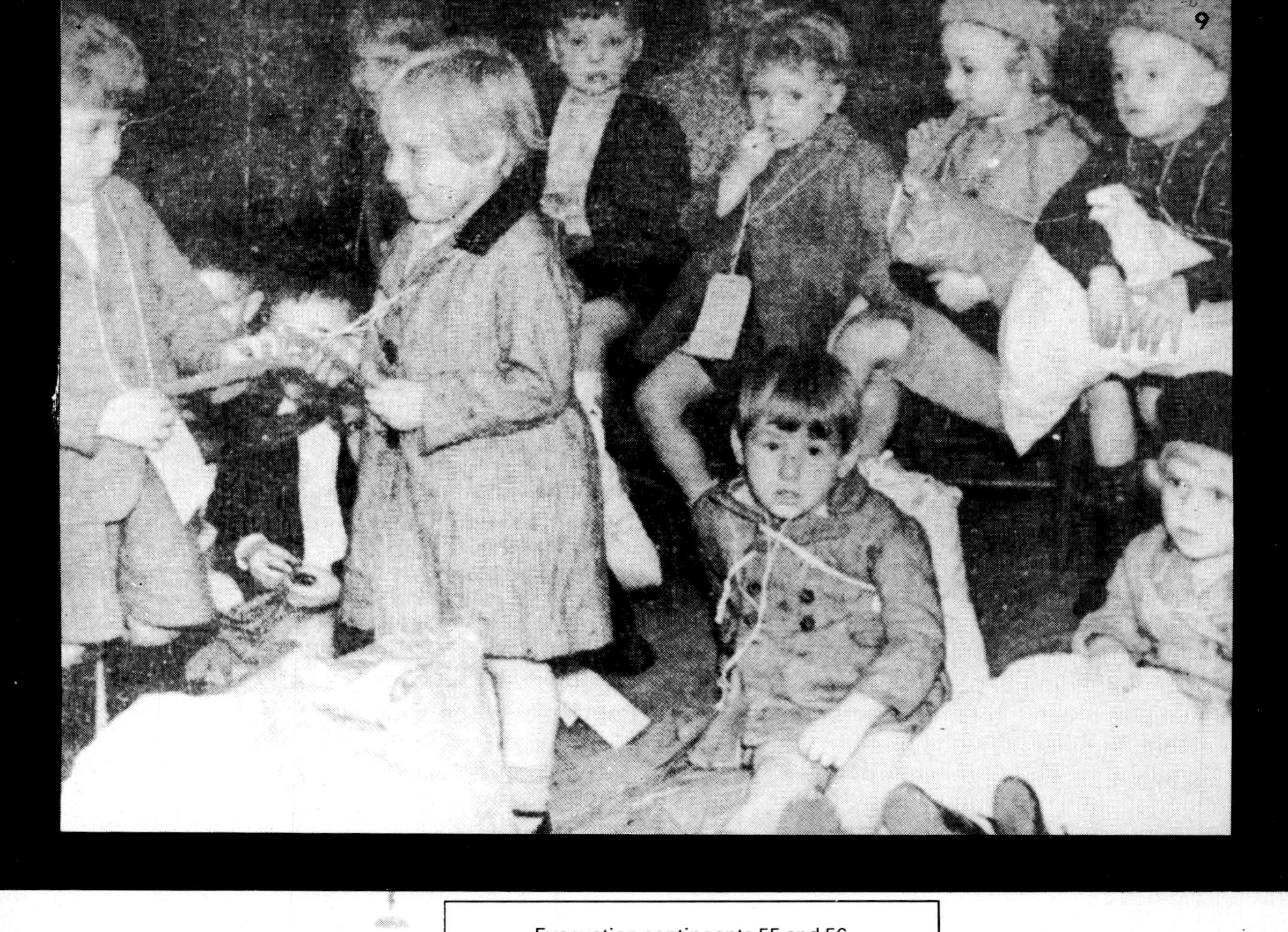
9

10

Evacuation contingents 55 and 56 leaving Salford.

11
12

Levenshulme Station.

New Moston Central School.

CIVIL DEFENCE

Mothers and young children wait at Levenshulme Station.

At the height of the bombing approximately 1½ million people in Britain were involved in Air Raid Precaution (ARP) work of which about 80% were part-time volunteers and nearly 25% women.

Most ARPs were Wardens whose job was essentially in two separate parts. He had to judge the extent and type of damage in his area so that the Control Centre could send the appropriate rescue services. His local knowledge was vital if time was to be saved hunting for survivors trapped beneath debris. Secondly, he was responsible for getting the "bombed-out" to some sort of shelter or a Rest Centre. Over 90% of wardens were part-timers and one in six was a woman. There were normally six wardens to a post, and one post to every 500 people.

First Aid Posts (FAPs) were usually manned by a doctor, a trained nurse and nursing auxiliaries. There was normally one FAP to every 15,000 people. There were also mobile units which could be called in to reinforce a hard pressed fixed post or even a hospital.

Under the orders of the Central Centre were the First Aid Parties. Each party consisted of four men and a driver. All were experienced first aid workers having been trained by either the Red Cross, St. John's Ambulance or the St. Andrew's Society. Their main task was to help the Rescue Men release trapped casualties and then to administer what aid they could before deciding whether or not a casualty needed further treatment at a post or hospital.

The task of the Rescue Men was the really back-breaking work in Civil Defence. Often amid fire and with the ever present danger of explosion from fractured gas pipes they searched the debris for both victims and survivors.

The ARP organisation embraced many others ranging from the Women's Voluntary Service (WVS), who in the early stages looked after the "bombed-out" as well as manning canteens and Rest Centres, to the police and fire services.

In the 1930's, Manchester already possessed a highly professional brigade which was under the direct control of the Chief Constable, the firemen subject to police conditions of service. Even so, the brigade could not be expected to answer all the emergencies resulting from a major air raid. So along with other towns and cities, Manchester raised an Auxiliary Fire Service (AFS).

AFS equipment usually consisted of trailer pumps for towing behind suitable vehicles, capable of delivering between 120gpm and 900gpm. Their fire engines (heavy units), were painted battleship grey and lacked the brass and chrome adornments of regular appliances. On the 30th August 1939, all AFS and regular units were issued with steel helmets and respirators and the Home Office announced that the weekly rates of pay for full-time AFS crews would be £3 for men, £2 for women, 25/- for youths aged 17/18 and £1 for youths aged 16-17.

In Manchester, 55 AFS Fire Stations were operational. Some of these were little more than factory loading bays, railway arches and requisitioned industrial premises. Many had no facilities whatsoever for the crews. Others like Crumpsall Hospital AFS were new buildings built out of prefabricated parts.

Members of Manchester Corporation ARP Committee on a tour of inspection of the underground sections of the Bridgewater Canal.

In December 1939, this massive air-raid siren was fitted on the roof of one of the stores in the city centre.

Roof spotters watch the sky over Manchester. September, 1940.

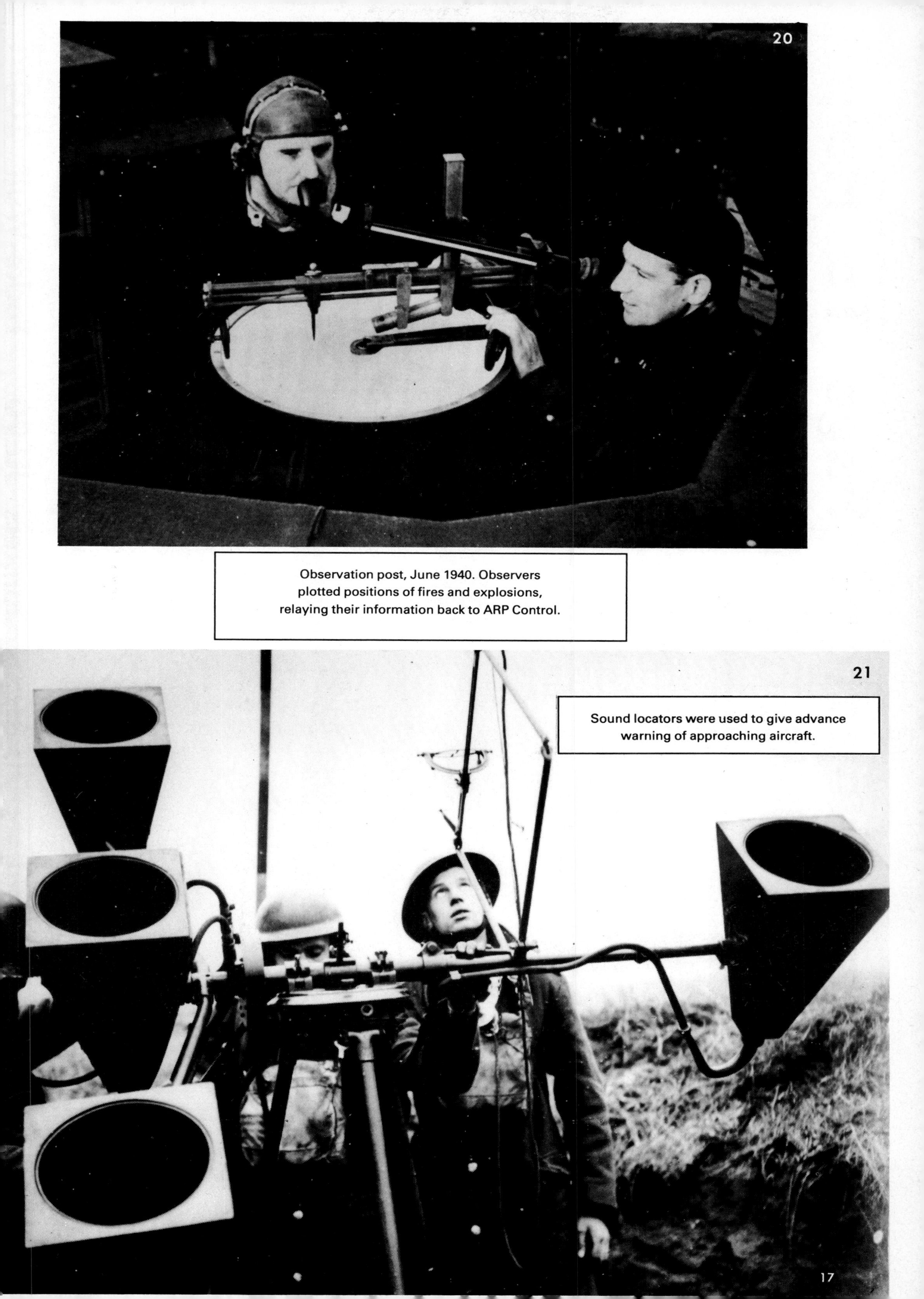

20

Observation post, June 1940. Observers plotted positions of fires and explosions, relaying their information back to ARP Control.

21

Sound locators were used to give advance warning of approaching aircraft.

A "Sunday Dispatch" Page To Help Everyone Defend The Country

THE War Office has issued these diagram pictures of enemy troop-carrying 'planes. They are intended to guide Local Defence Volunteers and all members of the public.

Some of these pictures have been published elsewhere in the past few days, but this page contains many more details and also silhouettes of comparable British bombers. It is the only complete chart. Cut it out and hang it on your wall.

If you see an aeroplane that resembles an enemy, tell the police, an air raid warden, or the L.D.V. at once.

Here are some simple points to remember:

If the 'plane has more than two engines it is *probably* a German.

The 3-engined Junkers Ju 52 has one engine in the nose, looking like the head of a fly. These have been the 'planes most used for parachutists.

The Junkers Ju 90 has wings that sweep backwards like a swallow in flight.

Note the square-cut edges of the wings and tails of the Junkers 'planes.

If a bomber is flying low in daylight, note the colour.

British bombers are mostly painted black on the underside. (There are some silver or light green.)

The badge painted on British 'planes is like a red, white, and blue target, with the red as the bull's-eye.

German bombers are painted light blue-grey under the fuselage and wings.

Their badge is a black cross, outlined with a white band. The white band itself is outlined in black.

A black swastika is usually carried on the tail of the 'plane.

THESE ARE THE TYPES OF GERMAN AIRCRAFT YOU ARE MOST LIKELY TO SEE

Junkers JU 52

Junkers JU 86

Junkers JU 90

Focke-Wulf 200

HERN ASSURANCE BUILDINGS
AIR RAID
PRECAUTIONS
23

24

ARP Wardens, Salford.

ARP Wardens, Eccles, 1940.

25

TO BLACKOUT CYCLISTS

COULD THIS BE YOU—TO-NIGHT?

It's not a silly question, you know. You may think that, just because you can see cars coming, their drivers can see you — *but that isn't true.* Blackout-time is danger-time. You must rely on one person in particular — yourself.

CYCLE **C-A-R-E-F-U-L-L-Y**

Issued by the Ministry of War Transport

TO BLACKOUT DRIVERS

28

THAT CYCLIST MAY HAVE SEEN YOU – BUT . . .

perhaps he didn't realize that under black-out conditions drivers cannot see much beyond the range of their lamps. You who drive at night must make allowances for other road users — you should *always* be able to pull up within the limits of your vision.

DRIVE **S-L-O-W-L-Y**

Issued by the Ministry of War Transport

AFS Messenger boy.

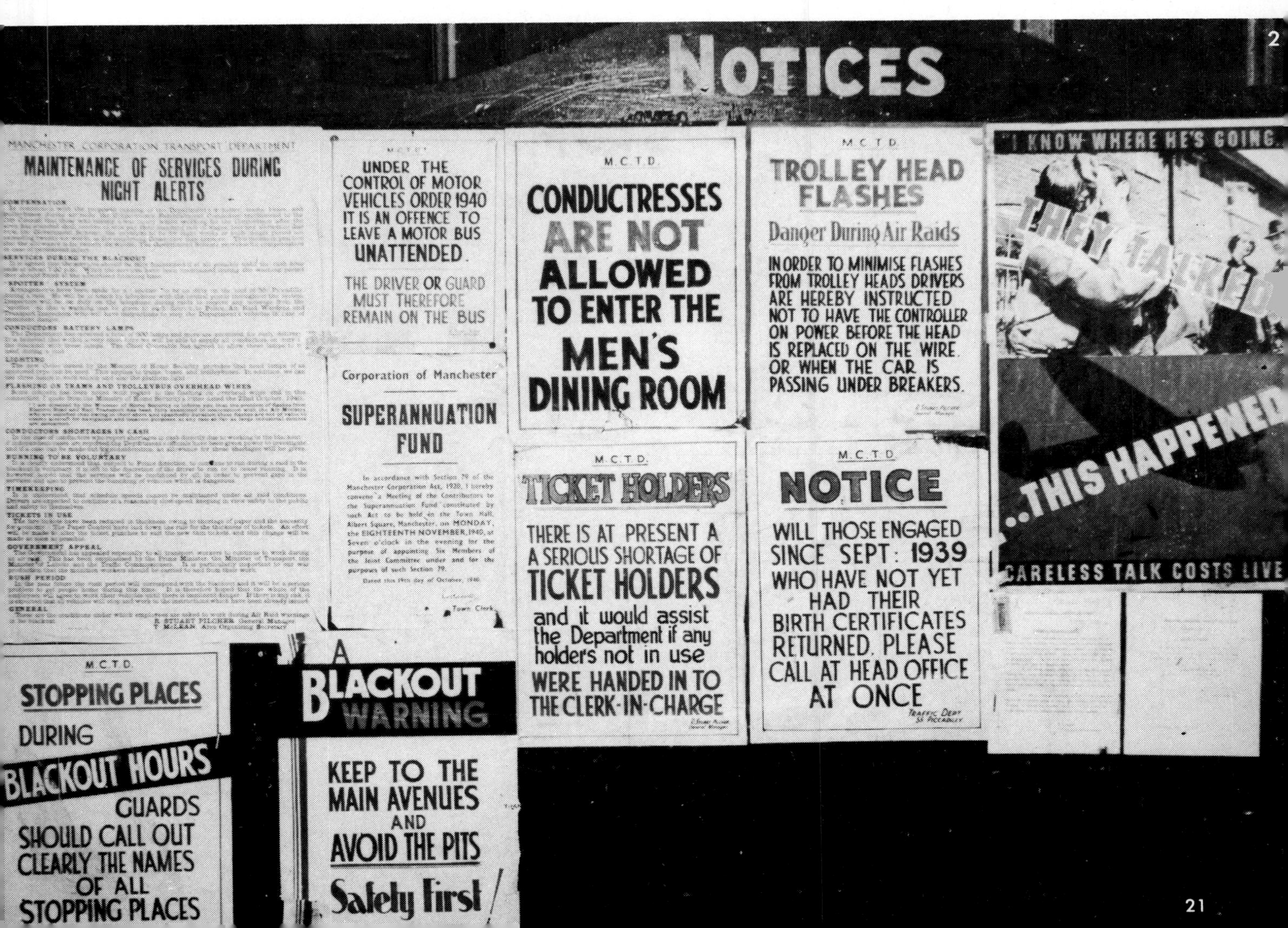

ARP Control Room at Manchester Ship Canal.

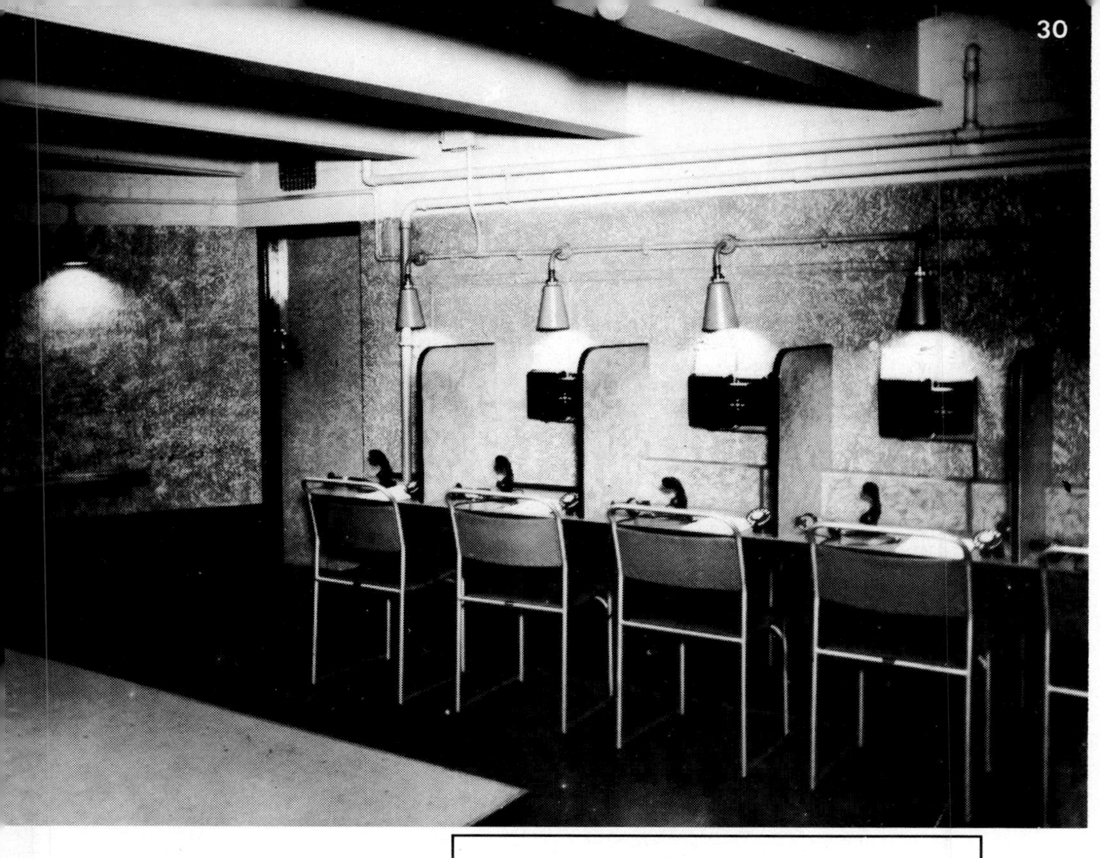

ARP Control Centre.

No. 27 Fire Force, Division F.
Fire Control Room, Manchester
Ship Canal Dock Office.

32

Two shots of a wrecked fire appliance in St. Mary's Gate. 24th December, 1940.

33

Area Training School at St. Joseph's, Longsight, the buildings were requisitioned in 1939.

34

Emergency Water Tank. 23rd December, 1940.

AFS fight the blaze in Portland Street during the Blitz

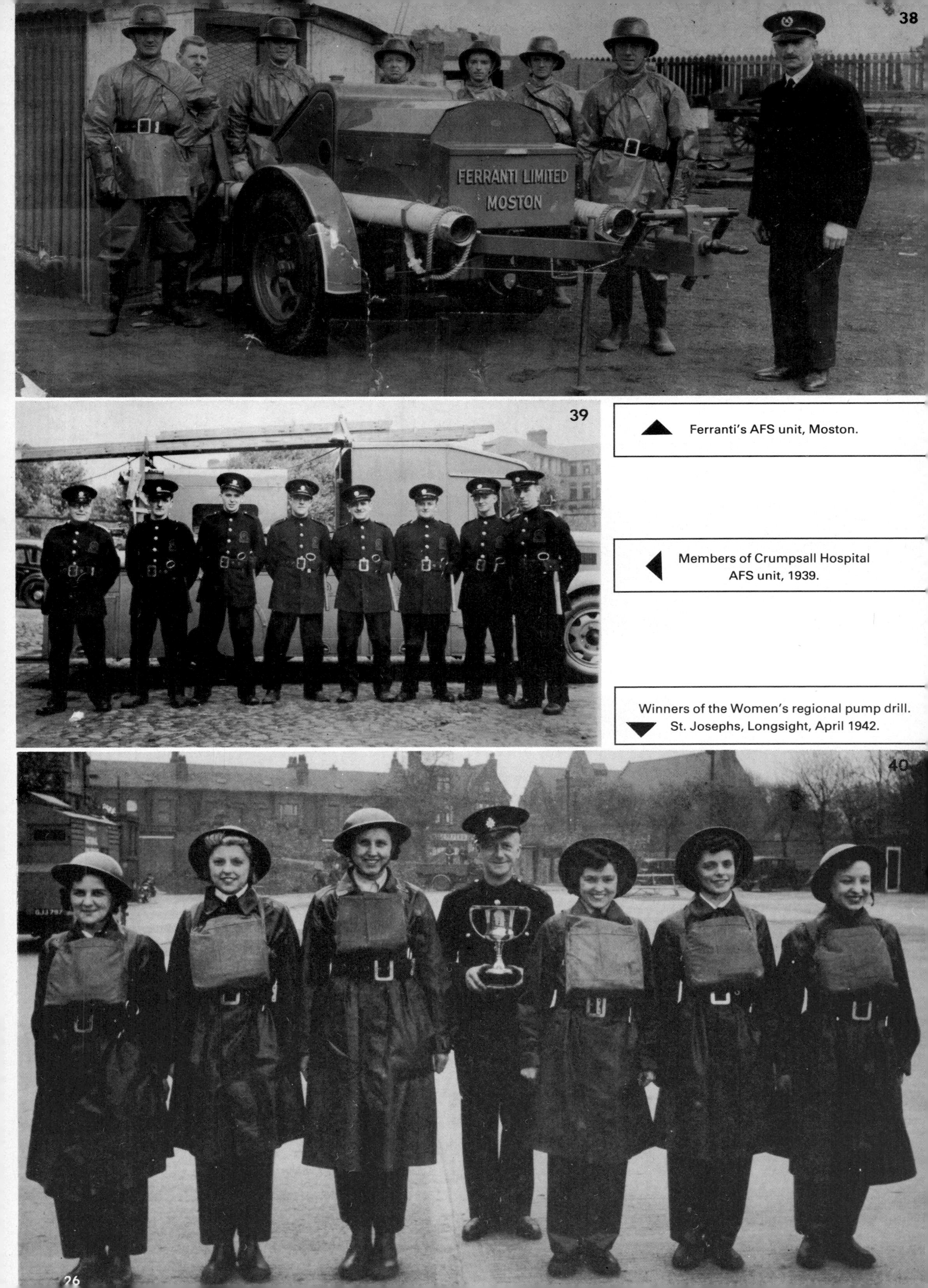

38

39

40

▲ Ferranti's AFS unit, Moston.

◀ Members of Crumpsall Hospital AFS unit, 1939.

Winners of the Women's regional pump drill.
▼ St. Josephs, Longsight, April 1942.

Anti-gas clothing.

AFS training at St. Josephs.

Manchester Corporation Transport's decontamination squad.

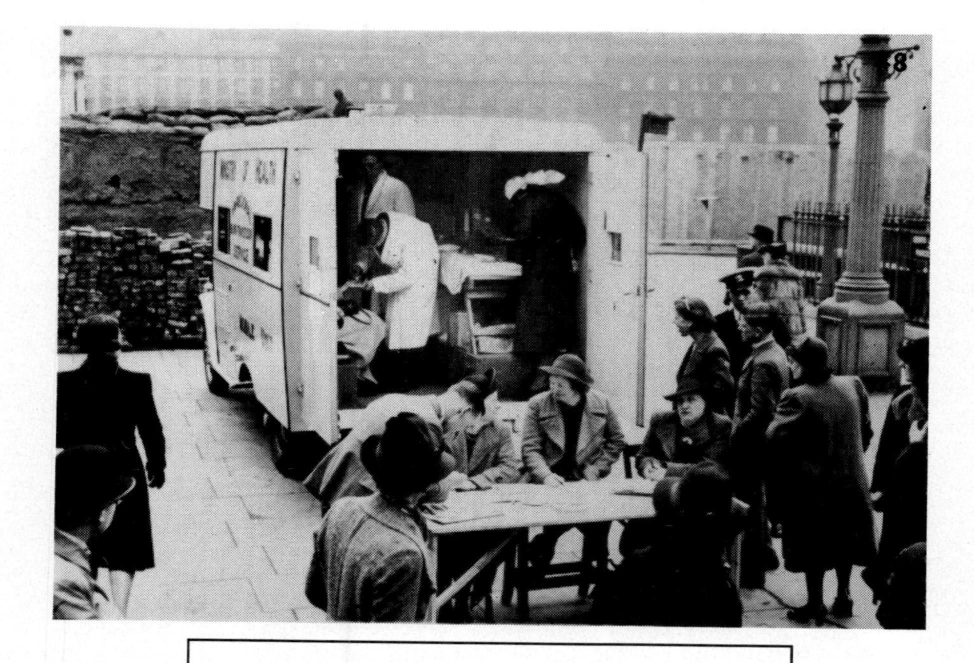

Blood transfusion service in Piccadilly.

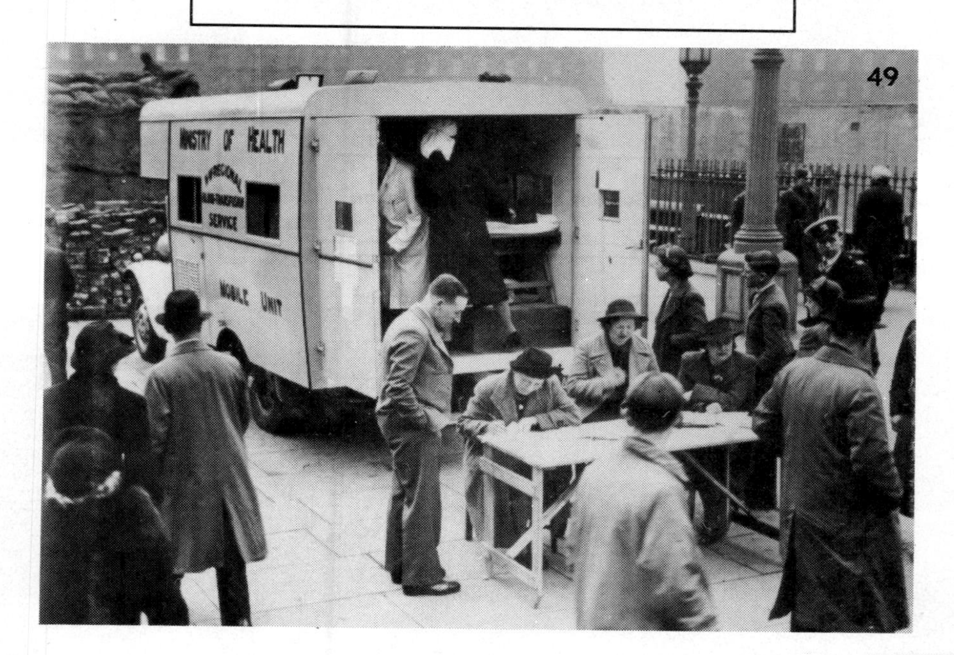

SHELTERS

Anderson Shelters

Named after Sir John Anderson, Secretary of State for Home Affairs, Anderson shelters became a familiar sight at the bottom of many a garden and examples survive to this day. They were cheap to produce and consisted of two corrugated steel walls which met in a ridge at the top and were then bolted to sturdy rails to give the structure strength. The shelter was then "planted" three feet into the ground and covered with at least eighteen inches of earth. The entrance was protected by a steel shield and a blast wall made of soil. Andersons were very effective and were capable of protecting up to six people from almost anything but a direct hit. In pic. 85, page 49, ARP workers are salvaging a gramaphone from a shelter that had been buried under several feet of debris after a bomb had dropped less than seven yards from the entrance. None of the four occupants were injured. However, there were problems with the early Andersons. They were too small to sleep in and more importantly they were prone to flooding. In December 1940, there were 39,320 Anderson shelters in the Manchester area. The Corporation together with a number of building contractors were working flat out relining, draining and waterproofing these Andersons but with winter well and truly set-in 10,000 still required urgent attention. Approximately 2,250,000 Andersons were distributed free of charge but in October 1939 a change in Government policy meant that any person earning over £5 a week had to buy their own at prices ranging from £6 14s to £10 18s each. Production ceased altogether in March 1940 due in-part to a steel shortage but also to the fact that the building of communal shelters was officially encouraged.

Morrison Shelters

Named after the Minister of Home Security, Herbert Morrison. Like the Anderson this type of shelter was designed for family use. Essentially the Morrison shelter looked like a steel table standing thirty-three inches high with sides of wire mesh. The unique feature was that Morrisons could be erected indoors.

Trench Shelters

First made their appearance in public parks during the Czech Crisis in 1938. At the beginning of the war, the Government ordered local authorities to make these shelters more permanent by lining the sides and roofing them with concrete or steel. These shelters were unpopular and were often impossible to keep dry.

Surface Shelters.

Introduced in March 1940, these were "communal" shelters of brick and cement and designed to protect up to fifty residents of a street or block of flats. However, because of a cement shortage, many of the early examples were built without mortar thus making them liable to collapse if hit by the pressure wave from a bomb blast. Ventilation was limited and even when chemical toilets were provided they could be unbearable!

Public Shelters

Surveys were undertaken in town centres to assess how many existing cellars and vaults could offer some means of protection to the general public in the event of air raids. Also brick and concrete public surface shelters were built and though similar in design to "communal" shelters they could accomodate many more people. Public surface shelters were built in Piccadilly. Shelters of this type often gained individual characteristics and some sort of social life developed - often with official support, with concerts, play readings, libraries, sing-songs and so on. The larger public shelters had full-time wardens and were equipped with first aid posts.

Surface shelters in Piccadilly.

63

Men of No.80 Detachment, 50th Lancs. Home Guard (Manchester Corporation Transport).

64

Salford Home Guard.

65

"D" Company Salford L.D.V. (circa 1940).

The Lord Bishop of Manchester conducts a drum head service at Manchester race course for the 43rd Lancs. Home Guard, 11th August, 1940.

70

Allotment in Piccadilly.

BUY NOW!
HENRYS
FOR XMAS GIFTS!
STILL AT MANCHESTERS' LOWEST PRICES...
ST. MARGARET'S ART SILK HOSE PERFECTS 1'11½
GAY TARTAN PARTY FROCKS 7'11
LADIES' RIPPLE CLOTH DRESSING GOWNS 7'11
SMART ART SILK HOUSE SMOCKS IN W.X. & O.S. 5'11
ALL - WOOL JUMPERS & CARDIGANS 7'11
LADIES' SUEDE HANDBAGS FLAP-OVER STYLE 7'6
Ladies' SLIPPERS Large VARIETY, MANY COLOURS 4'11
Children's ART SILK Quilted DRESSING GOWNS 6'6
MEN'S "JAEGER" ALL-WOOL SCARVES 2'11
MEN'S Double-Fronted TUNIC SHIRTS 2 COLLARS 5'-
IRISH LINEN SETTEE SETS FROM 6'11
"WHISTLING BOY" FIGURES COLOURED 2'11
21-PIECE TEA SETS SELF COLOUR 4'11
CHRISTMAS CARDS WITH ENVELOPES 6 IN BOX 6d.
★ FATHER CHRISTMAS IN TOYLAND THIRD FLOOR
HENRYS MARKET ST - MANCHESTER
Henrys Stores. Ltd.

"ONLY 30/- A WEEK TO FEED FIVE"
This real-life story is based on the actual experiences of an Oxted family whose name and address can be seen on personal application.
MRS K'S KIDDIES COULD DO WITH A BIT MORE FOOD.
YES, THEY'RE POORLY KIDS.
O-OH, I CAN'T BEAR IT- THEY MEAN OUR KIDS!
THEY SAID THE BOYS LOOK UNDERNOURISHED.
WELL, YOU KNOW AS WELL AS I DO THAT OUR BUDGET CAN'T BE CHANGED!
MRS. K'S WEEKLY BUDGET
Rent 10-6
Coal 4-4
Gas + electricity 3-6
Insurance 4-8
Clothes Club 3-0
Food 1-10-0
Sundries 1-0
Husband's exes. 3-0
£3-0-0
THAT NIGHT, IT KEPT HIM AWAKE
THINKS
THE INSURANCE COULD BE DOCKED - BUT WITH THE THREE KIDS TO THINK OF, I DAREN'T DO THAT... GOSH. - I KNOW, I'LL ASK OLD JOCK AT WORK ABOUT IT, IN THE MORNING HE'S GOT THREE KIDS, TOO.
NEXT EVENING, MRS. K. HEARS WHAT JOCK SAID
JOCK SHOWED ME THIS! LOOK WHAT IT SAYS: "Pre-digested cocoa is more nourishing in itself, helps children to digest all their other food and makes even the simplest meals go further." HOW'S THAT?
WELL, WE CAN HAVE A TRY AT IT.
SOME WEEKS LATER
I'M FULL RIGHT UP!
ME TOO, MUMMIE.
THEIR MEALS SATISFY THEM COMPLETELY EVER SINCE WE TRIED THIS PRE-DIGESTED COCOA.
MRS. K., YOUR BOYS DO GROW FAST. ARE THEY ON A TONIC?
NO, IT'S THAT SPECIAL PRE-DIGESTED COCOA- ROWNTREES. IT AIDS DIGESTION, AND MAKES EVERY MORSEL THEY EAT GO FURTHER!
Many other families are finding that
Rowntree's Cocoa makes every meal go further
ROWNTREE'S COCOA IS A FOOD made by a special "pre-digestive" process, so that it is not only more digestible and nourishing itself — it helps people to digest all their other food more quickly — and with less effort. This means children get more nourishment out of their meals — put on extra bone and muscle.
ROWNTREE'S COCOA HAS A LOVELY, RICH CHOCOLATY FLAVOUR. Half a teaspoonful makes one cup — so it's more economical than ordinary cocoa. And because it's "pre-digested," when taken before bed, Rowntree's Cocoa helps your supper to digest more easily — and so promotes deep, healthy sleep.
ROWNTREE'S COCOA AIDS DIGESTION
Still at pre-war prices — 6d. quarter lb., 11d. half lb.

73

WHY AREN'T THERE *MORE* TRAINS ?

Factories turning out guns, bombers and fighters depend on the Railways for supplies.

To keep them working at top pressure the Railways must run thousands of additional goods trains by day and night.

The Railways must also keep the Nation's food, coal and export trades moving.

Essential trains must have first claim on the lines. *It is as vital to ration trains as it is to ration food.* The Railways are giving you every passenger train the tracks will take.

WE'LL BEAT HITLER BY HELPING ONE ANOTHER

BRITISH RAILWAYS

75

WAR-FARE

COOKERY DEMONSTRATIONS

IN COLLABORATION WITH THE NATIONAL FOOD CAMPAIGN

at the GAS SHOWROOMS, TOWN HALL, MANCHESTER

EACH MONDAY AND THURSDAY, AT 2-30 p.m.

TO-MORROW (Thursday)—CHRISTMAS FOR THE CHILDREN

NEXT WEEK—

MONDAY, 16th DECEMBER	THURSDAY, 19th DECEMBER—
FILMS FEATURING FOOD FACTS	ENTERTAINING "EXTRAS"

CITY OF MANCHESTER GAS DEPARTMENT

— GO TO IT —

In 1936, the go ahead was given to electrify the Manchester-Sheffield mainline. In December 1939, the project was deferred for the duration of the war even though 50 per cent of the civil engineering work had been completed. Several miles of catenary had been erected as well as a new locomotive depot at Darnell.

Pic. 74 shows troops digging out a train in February 1940. Even the snow-plough is stuck. One of the overhead catenary is in the background.

7

To help alleviate fuel shortages, Manchester experimented with gas-producing equipment, the white stripes were painted so that the trailer would be visable in the blackout.

A Manchester Corporation bus in wartime red and grey livery.

THE BOMBING

In June 1939, the Luftwaffe began a major reconnaissance of the United Kingdom with priority being given to possible industrial, economic and communications targets. Thousands of factories, mines, chemical plants, textile mills, railway sidings, bridges power stations, water and sewage works were individually indentified and plotted on to pirated copies of Ordnance Survey Maps.

By the end of October 1940, the Luftwaffe were not having things entirely their own way. The Blitz on London was developing into a war of attrition, proving costly both in crews and aircraft, yet there was no sign of a British surrender, or a willingness to discuss an armistice, only a stiffening of resolve. The Luftwaffe's operational bomber strength had been whittled away to just over 700 planes and though new aircraft were being delivered to their front line squadrons there was a shortage of spares due to the fact that the German aircraft industry was still working peace time shifts.

By the beginning of November, the situation had deteriorated even further and Goering was forced to call off large scale daylight attacks. In his new directive to his Air Fleets, Goering stated that though London would remain the priority target, the Luftwaffe would also turn its attention to the industrial areas of Britain.

It was a few minutes after 7.00pm on the night of the 14th November when the air raid sirens warned the citizens of Coventry of impending attack. When the all clear sounded eleven hours later, a third of the city centre had been completely destroyed. In all, an estimated 1200 High Explosive (HE) bombs, 50 parachute mines and 30,000 incendiaries had been dropped on the city. In Germany, a new word was coined, meaning the destruction of a city from the air - "Coventrated".

Before the end of November, Liverpool, Southampton and Birmingham had been subjected to heavy raids. In December, the weather conditions were such that for fifteen nights the Luftwaffe were unable to get into the air. However, there were eleven major raids and five moderately heavy attacks. London suffered three major attacks and twelve light raids. Sheffield was attacked twice and Liverpool, Birmingham, Portsmouth and Leicester were Blitzed.

It was during this period that Manchester suffered two of its heaviest attacks. At 6.38pm, on the night of the 22nd December, the sirens wailed their ominous warning across the city. Within two minutes, incendaries were falling on and around Albert Square and a building on the corner of Princess Street and Clarence Street soon caught fire. Incendiaries were also reported in the area around Bridgewater Street. The main threat seemed to be developing in the vicinty of Deansgate, where the top of the Royal Exchange was ablaze. Fire had taken hold of Victoria Buildings and a fractured gas main outside Hailwood's Creamery in St. Mary's Gate was alight. To add to the already mounting problems for the emergency services was the fact that 200 men and 30 pumps were still in Liverpool where they had been sent the night before to reinforce that city's hard pressed firefighters. By 8.00pm, the Exchange Hotel was well and truly on fire and shops in Market Street were threatened. Part of Victoria Buildings had collapsed into Deansgate, blocking the thoroughfare from Blackfriars Street to Victoria Bridge and the road to Salford became blocked when a building at the corner of Bridge Street and Gartside Street also collapsed. In Portland Street, Sackville Street and Watson Street, fires rampaged through a number of warehouses and a cluster of HE bombs fell on the Oxford Road area, including Gray Street, Stafford Street and Cooke Street. There were some lucky escapes. Some 450 people who had taken refuge in Gibson's shelter in Erskine Street had become trapped by debris - all were saved. In another incident, a HE bomb scored a direct hit on a shelter in St. George's Park, but by pure chance there was no-one in it at the time.

At 7.15pm on the 23rd the sirens sounded again. When the all clear was given at 1.29am the following morning the city had been subjected to heavy incendiary attack; an estimated 55 HE bombs had exploded. Rescue Parties had attended 501 incidents and pulled 226 people out alive from the rubble. Additional fire-fighting cover came from the London Fire Brigade who sent 300 officers, men and women, with a convoy of 40 pumps, 7 hose lorries and 6 canteen vans. By 3.00am on the morning of the 24th the fires were contained though many were still burning furiously. Then fate took a hand. A strong wind blew up carrying sparks and burning embers. The fire spread, dangerously out of control and the Piccadilly area was threatened. A wall of fire extended from Moseley Street, across Piccadilly and beyond Portland Street. In depth it threatened to penetrate as far as Princess Street. There was little alternative but to call in the Royal Engineers to blast fire breaks.

Within a mile of Albert Square, 31.3 acres were in ruins, 165 warehouses, 150 offices, 5 banks and 200 other business premises were destroyed or severly damaged and 300 warehouses, 220 offices, 20 banks and 500 other business premises damaged to a lesser degree. 30,000 houses had been damaged and 5,049 people had been made homeless. The "bombed-out" were distributed between 28 rest centres. By the end of the 2nd January 1941, 13,000 houses had been repaired and only 1,600 people remained at the rest centres, which in an eight day period had managed to provide 72,000 meals.

The effects of the two nights on Salford were heavy. Some 276 HE bombs and 10,000 incendiaries had landed on the city causing 1 conflagration, 31 major fires and 400 large or medium fires. Fire fighting cover for the city had been stretched to the limit and reinforcements had been called in from 59 outside brigades. 8,000 houses were destroyed or damaged together with 15 schools. Civilian casualties were 197 killed, 177 seriously injured and 648 slightly injured. Eighteen members of the police, fire and civil defence services had been killed and 85 injured.

At Stretford, 12,000 houses had been destroyed or damaged and 2,000 people made homeless.

Electricity supplies to the ARP Report Centre were interupted for two periods amounting to four hours. A direct hit on the East Union Police Station destroyed the telephone link and cut off the Report Centre from the reserve ambulance depot at Empress Road. Communications with the Wright Street Rescue Party Depot and Manchester Town Hall were also severed. Stretford ARP services were reduced to relying on bicycle messengers and runners. In all 106 civilians were killed, 87 seriously wounded and 184 slightly wounded.

Next to the two-night Blitz, the third heaviest raid occured on the night of the 1st/2nd June 1941. In an attack lasting 90 minutes, major fires and considerable damage was caused in the Derby Street, Oldham Street and Southall Street areas. Among the buildings damaged were the Assize Courts, the Gaiety theatre, the Y.M.C.A., Police Headquarters in South Street and the College of Technology. Salford was hit hard and amongst the casualties were fourteen nurses who were killed at the Salford Royal Hospital.

The Luftwaffe's last major assault on the city occurred on Christmas Eve 1944. With their V1 launch sites either over run or flattened by heavy air attacks, the Germans had taken to launching these weapons from the air by Heinkel He 111s. With one of these flying bombs carried under the wing root, a He 111 proved to be exceedingly vulnerable and the units concerned (KG3'Blitz' and KG53'Legion Kondor') suffered heavy losses to our night-fighters. The V1 attack on Manchester was a failure. Only one flying bomb reached the city, one came down in the Goyt Valley but 27 people were killed when another dropped on Oldham.

Christmas 1940.

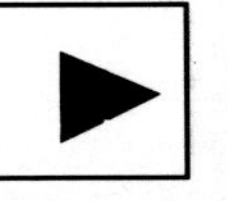

Fires rage in Market Street and Victoria Buildings. In the distance (top right of picture) Exchange Street Station is ablaze.

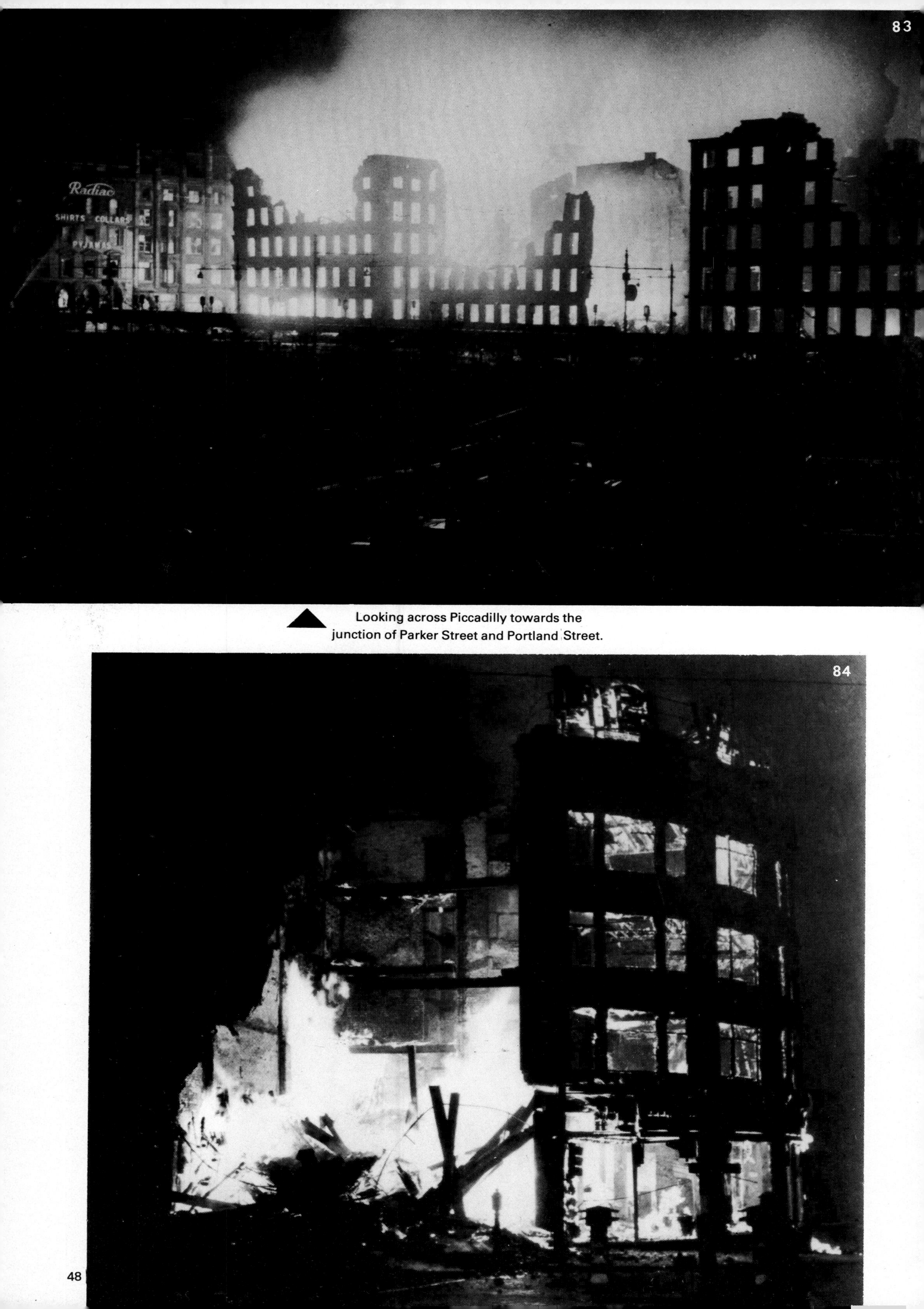

Looking across Piccadilly towards the junction of Parker Street and Portland Street.

85

A lucky escape from an Anderson shelter

86

A turntable ladder fire appliance at work outside the Daily Mail office, Deansgate.

87

CITY OF MANCHESTER.

This accommodation is reserved for a bombed-out family, and the Manchester Emergency Committee therefore appeal to all Citizens to co-operate with them in protecting the premises against wilful damage. Any persons damaging or entering upon the premises will be prosecuted.

Enquiries and information should be addressed to the Director of Housing, Town Hall, Manchester, 2.

R. H. ADCOCK,
Town Clerk.

88

Homeless on Christmas Day 1940.

Air raid damage, Piccadilly, Parker Street and Mosley Street Area.

Looking across the old Market Place towards the Shambles.

Piccadilly looking from Lewis's towards Portland Street.

The bombed-out ruins of Victoria Buildings in the course of demolition.

94 Manchester Assizes gutted by fire.
2nd June, 1941.

95 Crown Court.

96 View from the tower.

97 View from the tower.

Prime Minister Winston Churchill visits the ruins of Manchester Free Trade Hall.

Damage to Manchester Cathedral.

The ruins of Manchester Cathedral. The statue of Humphrey Chetham and his boy remains intact.

Wreckage in the Shambles.

102

103

Whilst sheltering under Greengate Bridge, Salford, this bus was completely destroyed when a bomb exploded directly above it.

104

Bomb damage at Exchange Street Station.

Exchange Street Station after repairs.

106

Exchange Street Station ablaze on Monday, 23rd December, 1940. This photograph was banned from publication by the censor.

Victoria Station on the morning of Tuesday, 24th December, 1940. This photograph was banned from publication by the censor.

East Market Street, Salford. Salford Town Hall on the left.

Surface shelter under construction, Piccadilly Station approach. Note the sign.

Bomb damage at Manchester United's ground. Until repairs were carried out, United played at Manchester City's ground, Maine Road.

Pic 117 shows the top of a parachute mine that dropped through the roof of 32 Dulcie Street, Chorlton-on-Medlock during the raid of 23rd December, 1940. Pic 118 shows the rest of the mine embedded in the cellar. The length of the mine was 10½ feet.

119

The Autodrill automatically drilled two holes into an unexploded bomb's casing. Once drilled, steam was inserted into the holes to melt away the explosive charge.

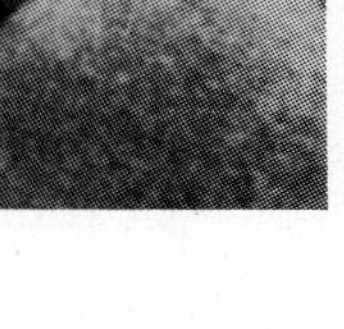

On Chirstmas Eve 1944, the Luftwaffe launched a V1 attack against Manchester. Though the attack failed, a bomb did come down in Oldham killing 27 people.

Luftwaffe Target photograph of Manchester and Salford Docks.

INDUSTRY AT WAR

The industrial might of Manchester and the surrounding area played a vital part in the nation's war effort. Hundreds of firms, large and small alike, were called upon to divert much of their capacity to meeting the emergency to such an extent that in individual companies it accounted for anything up to 95 per cent of output. Such is the complexity of this subject that in a book of this type we can give only a brief insight into the contribution made.

War was declared on Germany on the 3rd September 1939 and the firms in Trafford Park began to turn over to the production of munitions and armaments. The employment in the Park grew from about 50,000 to 75,000 people. Factories which previously had had no knowledge of areoplanes, tanks, guns, explosives, bombs or other munitions of war found themselves manufacturing components or undertaking final assemblies. Trafford Park became an arsenal. The importance of Trafford Park as a centre of wartime industry continued to grow. In December 1940, for three nights prior to Christmas Day, it was attacked by strong formations of enemy aircraft which did great damage. One of the companies, the Port of Manchester Warehouses Ltd., lost 11 of their 24 warehouses which amounted to a loss of 60 per cent of its storage capacity. Undaunted by the loss of roofs and surrounded by ruins, the men and women continued to work in the open.

In 1934, Metropolitan Vickers (Metrovick), one of the leading firms in Trafford Park, were awarded their first of several Admiralty contracts for signalling equipment. As rearmament got underway, Metrovick were contracted to produce radar equipment for air defence and to undertake the conversion of 18-pounder field guns into 25-pounders for the army as well as the manufacture of mountings for a new 4.5 inch anti-aircraft gun.

In July 1938, Metrovick were asked to build heavy bomber aircraft in conjuction with A.V. Roe & Co. Metrovick were to build a new plant on vacant land at Trafford Park with an output of two bombers a week. Construction work began in April 1939 and within six months the machine shop was operational. The bomber, aptly named the "Manchester", needed 26,000 jigs and tools. The first air-frame was ready for assembly in November 1940, passing final inspection on the 20th December. Then disaster struck. On the 23rd December, Trafford Park was Blitzed and the completed aircraft, together with twelve others under construction, was destroyed. Manufacture of the "Manchester" lasted until May 1941, when production was switched to the Lancaster bomber. In July 1943, the Lancaster was replaced by the Lincoln.

Metrovick's work in steam turbines led in 1938 to an Air Ministry enquiry for gas turbines. The Royal Aircraft Establishment at Farnborough collaborated on the project, the first completed plant being tested in October 1940. In 1940, the Ministry of Aircraft Production asked Metrovick to develop an axial-flow jet engine. This engine became known as the F2 and was first tested in December 1941. After modifications, it passed a 25 hour special category test in November 1942. A pair of these engines were installed in a specially modified Gloster F9/40 aircraft which was test flown on the 13th November 1943. On the 29th June 1943, a Lancaster bomber flew with an F2/1 jet engine housed in its tail. Development ultimately led to the F2/4 which had a rated thrust of 3,500lbs and a research model which could run on diesel fuel. Metrovick's work included generators, transformers, switchgear and power controls for anti-aircraft and naval guns. Other work included 35 mobile power stations for the Soviet Union, degaussing equipment to combat the magnetic mine and the development of "steaming out" equipment used for dealing with unexploded bombs.

On the 22nd October 1939, the Ford Motor Co. were asked to locate, build, equip and manage what became known as the Shadow Factory, at Eccles, for the mass production of the Rolls-Royce Merlin XX aero engine. Ford's expertise at mass production was urgently required, but it was vitally important that parts from the engines they built could be interchanged with engine parts manufactured at Roll-Royce plants.

To begin with, part of the old Ford factory at Trafford Park was turned into a tool-room, and machine-tools, technicians and draughtsmen, armed with Rolls-Royce blueprints, were sent north from Dagenham to make a start. By September 1940, three of the Shadow Factory buildings were complete and by the end of the year 2,300 workers had been recruited. In June 1941, the first 5 engines were built, at a cost of £5,640 each, and regular delivery to aircraft manufacturers started in August. In March 1942, the Air Ministry asked for production to be stepped up from 400 to 600 engines a month, plus 14 per cent in spares. By March 1942, productivity had increased to such an extent that the cost per engine was brought down to £2,484. In April 1944, the workforce stood at 17,307, of which 5,828 were women, turning out on average 900 engines a month. The total number of engines made at the factory was 30,428.

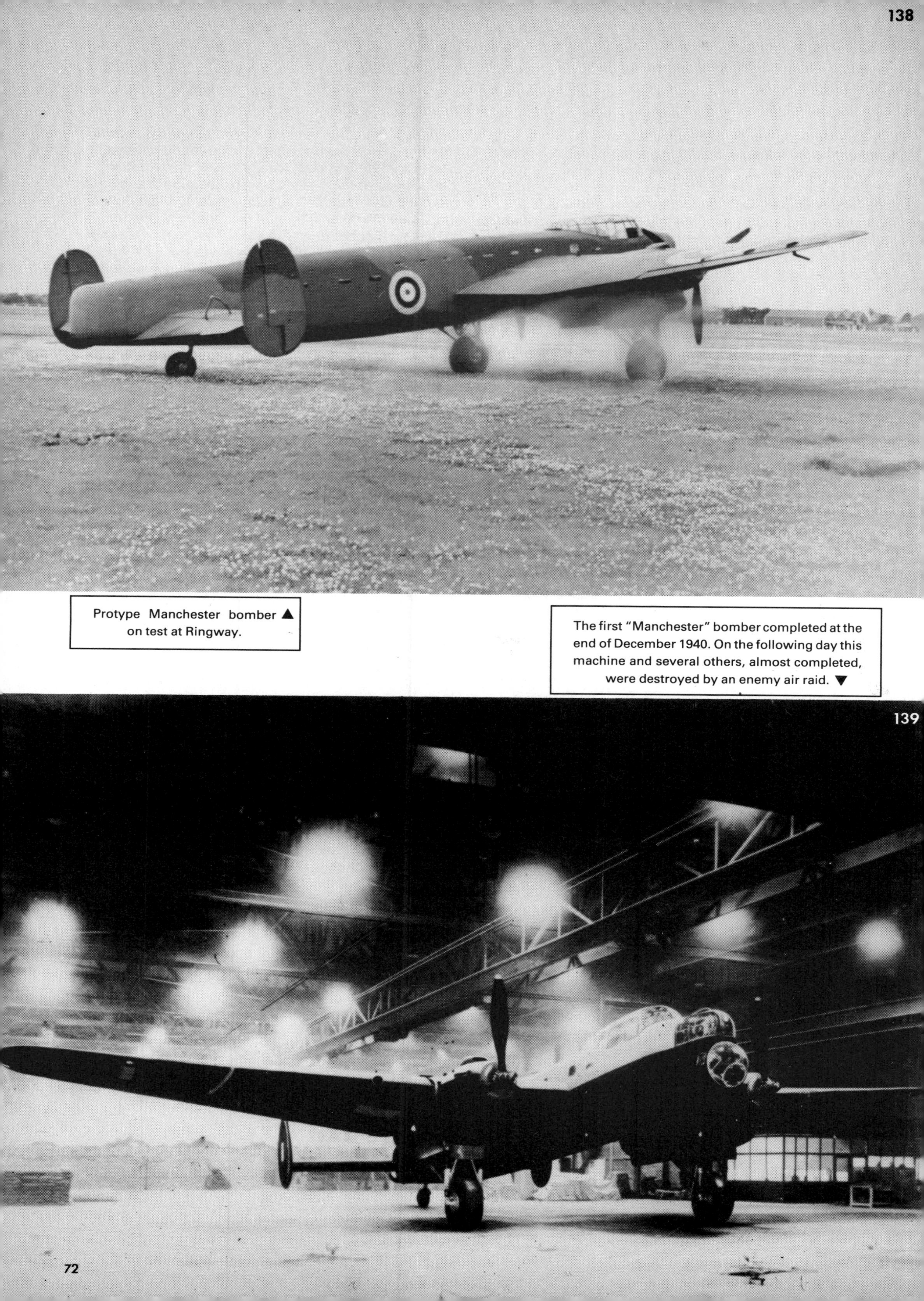

Protype Manchester bomber ▲
on test at Ringway.

The first "Manchester" bomber completed at the end of December 1940. On the following day this machine and several others, almost completed, were destroyed by an enemy air raid. ▼

139

General view of the bay for erecting centre sections of the "Lancaster" Bomber - Metrovicks.

Lancaster production at Avro.

142

Avro Lancaster on test at Woodford.

1

MAY 31ST.

THE CREW OF
'S FOR SUGAR'
WILL VISIT THE AIRCRAFT
FACTORY TO TELL YOU
OF SOME OF THEIR EXPERIENCES.
BE IN THE CANTEEN DURING
YOUR USUAL LUNCH HOUR BREAK.

PILOT OFFICER T.M.SCHOFIELD, FLIGHT OFFICER E.M.HAMILTON-NAVIGATO
SGT. H.BURGESS-FLIGHT ENGINEER, FLIGHT SGT. S.E.FUGUES-BOMB AIMER,
FLIGHT SGT. K.STEWART, SGT. K.J.WELLS & FLIGHT SGT. R.HILLAS WIRELESS OPERA

YOU BUILD THEM-THEY FLY THEM

ROLL UP IN YOUR THOUSANDS AND GIVE
THESE BOYS THE WELCOME THEY DESERVE

144

Lancaster bomber fitted with an F2/1 jet engine in the tail.
Note the air-intake above the fuselage.

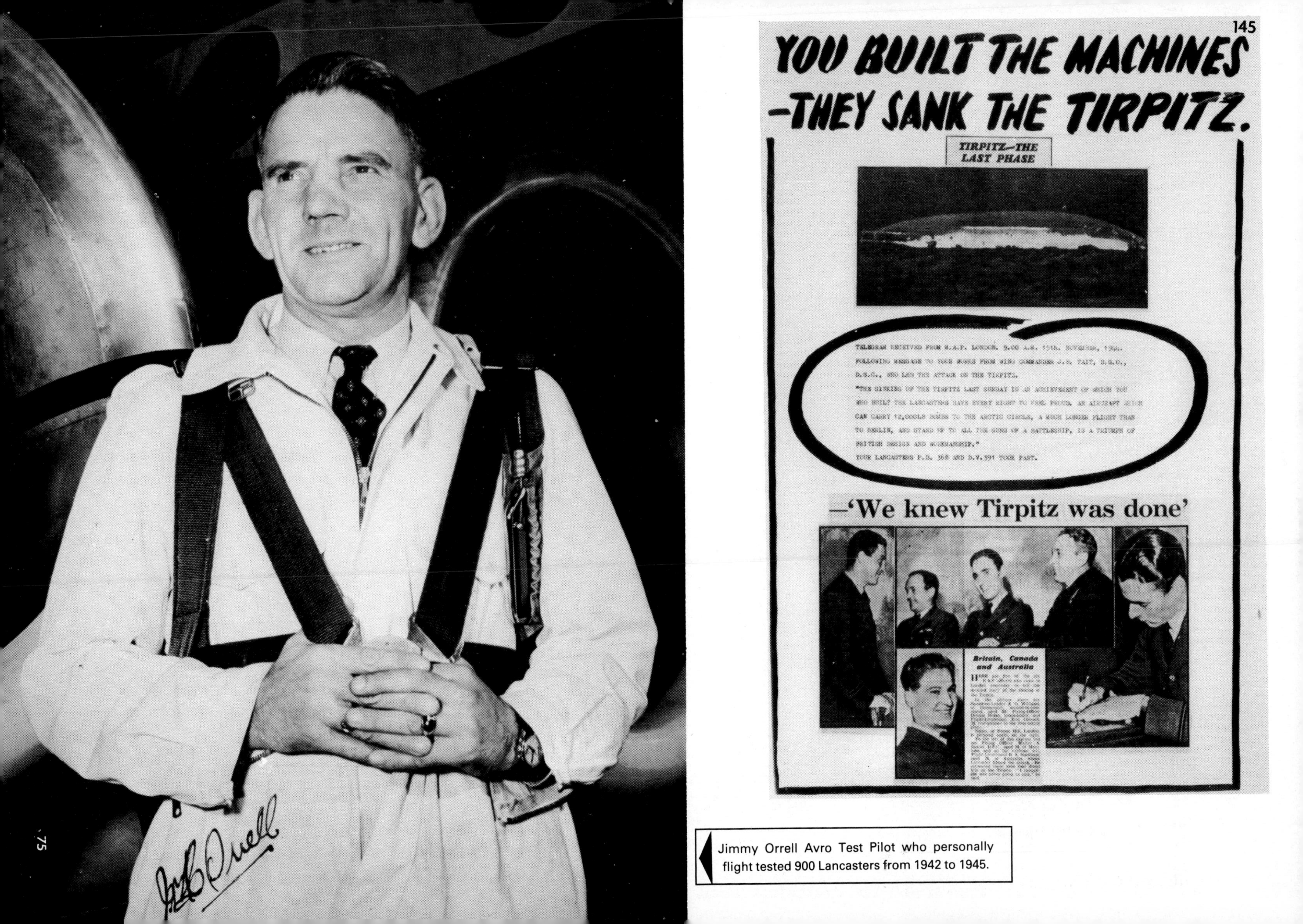

145

YOU BUILT THE MACHINES -THEY SANK THE TIRPITZ.

TIRPITZ—THE LAST PHASE

TELEGRAM RECEIVED FROM M.A.P. LONDON. 9.00 A.M. 15th. NOVEMBER, 1944.
FOLLOWING MESSAGE TO YOUR WORKS FROM WING COMMANDER J.B. TAIT, D.S.O., D.F.C., WHO LED THE ATTACK ON THE TIRPITZ.

"THE SINKING OF THE TIRPITZ LAST SUNDAY IS AN ACHIEVEMENT OF WHICH YOU WHO BUILT THE LANCASTERS HAVE EVERY RIGHT TO FEEL PROUD. AN AIRCRAFT WHICH CAN CARRY 12,000LB BOMBS TO THE ARCTIC CIRCLE, A MUCH LONGER FLIGHT THAN TO BERLIN, AND STAND UP TO ALL THE GUNS OF A BATTLESHIP, IS A TRIUMPH OF BRITISH DESIGN AND WORKMANSHIP."

YOUR LANCASTERS P.D. 368 AND D.V.391 TOOK PART.

—'We knew Tirpitz was done'

Britain, Canada and Australia

Jimmy Orrell Avro Test Pilot who personally flight tested 900 Lancasters from 1942 to 1945.

Merlin engines under construction at the Ford Shadow Factory.

149

Spitfire paid for by Manchester Corporation Transport. ▶

150a

▲ Spitfire presented to the RAF by the workers at Ferranti. This aircraft flew with a Polish Squadron.

Spitfire bought for the RAF by members of Manchester's Civil Defence. ▼

150b

A Royal visit and a Royal welcome to Metrovicks, May 1940.

153

▲ King George visits the Avro Factory at Newton Heath, 1939.

Royal visit May 1940. ▼

154

▲Anthony Eden inspects Metrovick's AFS unit.

Sir Felix Pole inspects members of Metrovick's National Fire Service unit.▼

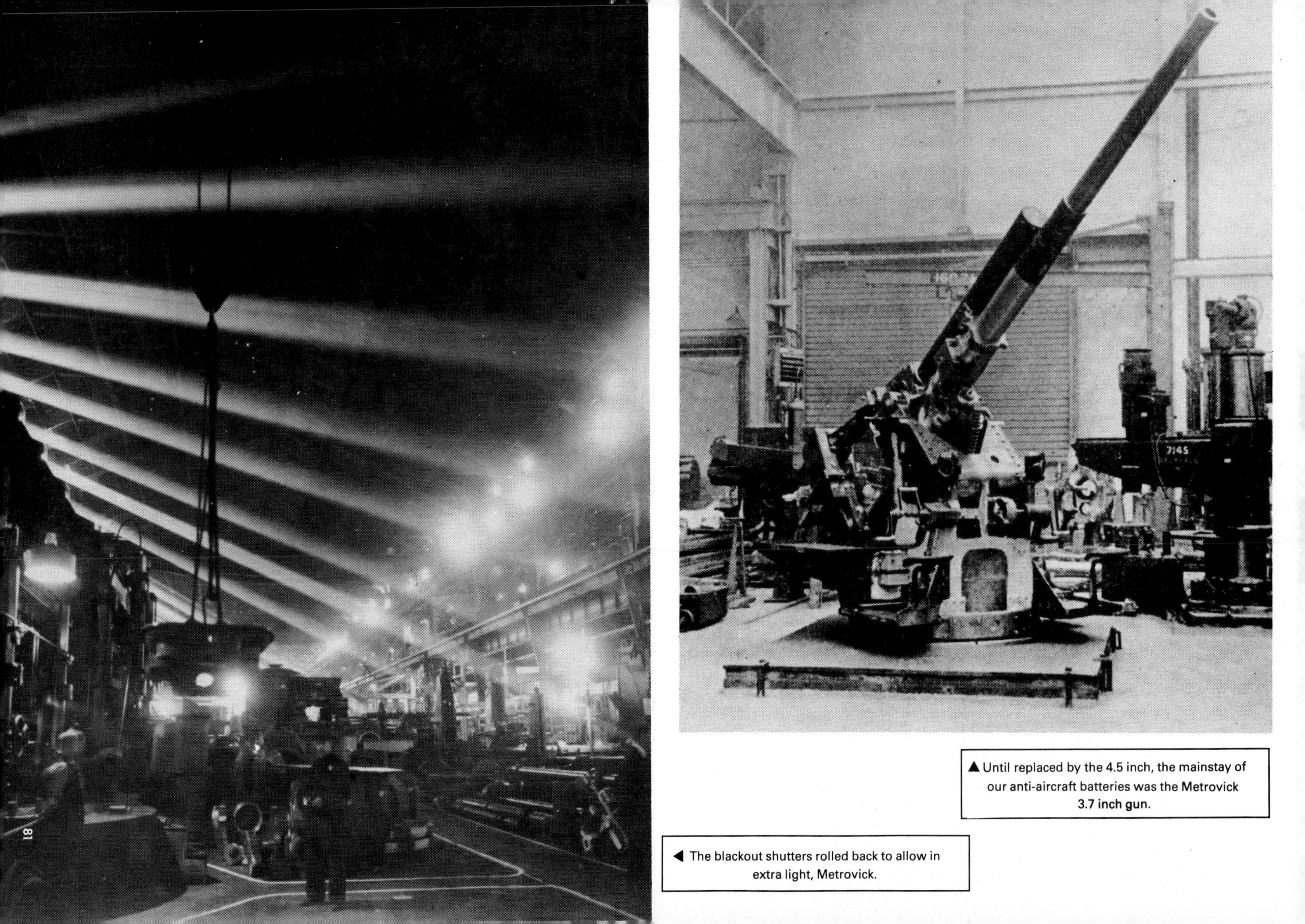

▲ Until replaced by the 4.5 inch, the mainstay of our anti-aircraft batteries was the Metrovick **3.7 inch gun**.

◀ The blackout shutters rolled back to allow in extra light, Metrovick.

159

▲ Mobile radar units built by Metrovick.

160

Work on Boxing Day

THERE will be no public holiday on Christmas Day in Scotland or on Boxing Day in England, Wales and Northern Ireland. Banks will remain open.

War workers are asked to take one day off only—either on Christmas Day or New Year's Day, and there will be no extra travel facilities over the holiday period.

The Ministry of Labour last night said that British arms production was increasing despite enemy efforts, and this was not the moment for any slackening off.

"So that production may be continued with as little interruption as possible and that the maximum amount of freight may be handled no additional services or facilities for passenger travel by road or rail can be provided

"Normal Sunday services will be run."

Industrial agreements relating to Bank Holidays will not be affected by the cancellation.

Official visit to Metrovick of Vice-Admiral Sir Harold Brown (fifth from left), Director of Munitions Production, Ministry of Supply. ▼

161

162

▲150cm mobile searchlight built by Metrovick.

Anti-tank gun assembly at Simon Engineering. ▼

163

164

FORT PERROT

▲ A mobile transformer built by Ferranti for ARP use. These transformers were designed so that power supplies could be quickly restored to bombed areas.

1000lb bomb crater in the aircraft factory Metrovick. ▼

168

Women workers at Manchester Corporation Transport, Hyde Road.

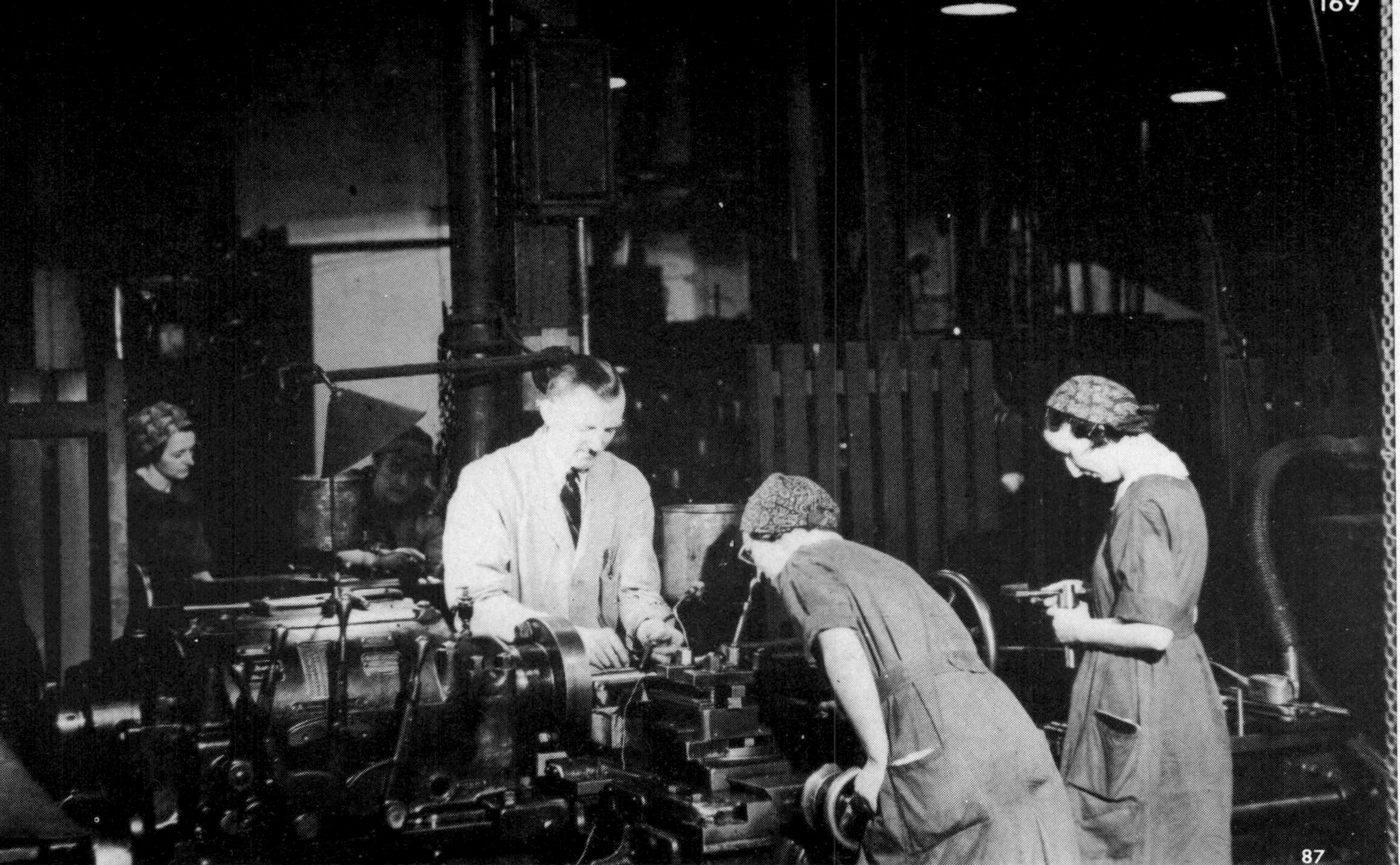
169

Linking Glover & Co. with Trafford Wharf, this gantry was built to allow the continuous loading of pipeline used on the "Pluto" project. "Pluto" was an undersea fuel line linking Britain with the Normandy beacheads.

THIS is the Food Fact we must NEVER forget!

Your bread costs ships.
Eat home-grown potatoes instead!

NO MORE BANANAS FOR BRITAIN

By Daily Mail Reporter

BANANAS will be banned from Britain as from the end of December.

The reason? They are too big.

An official of the Ministry of Food said yesterday: "Bananas are a bulky cargo compared with other food. Oranges, for instance, have far greater vitamin value than bananas—and occupy far less space.

"We want to use ships for more important cargoes than bananas."

The great Banana Ban—which hits grim truth in the words of the old song, "Yes, we have no Bananas"—burst like a bombshell in Covent Garden.

An official of the Colonial Office walked into the London offices of the biggest banana importers in the world and said: "I am sorry, but no more licences for the importation of bananas will be issued."

The prohibition will throw over a thousand men out of work in this country, and seriously affect the economic position of Jamaica, whose banana trade represents over half of the island's total exports.

Messrs. Elders and Fyffes, the importers, are protesting to the Government.

"We thought it might be because the Government required our ships," an official said, "but we were informed that there is no shortage of ships.

"While bananas are just commercial to us, they are a real, nourishing, honest-to-goodness food for women and children."

Before the war this country consumed 45,000,000 bananas a week, but war-time restrictions have reduced that by about half. In 1938 Jamaica shipped us £2,100,000 worth.

174

No.9 Dock. Note the number of guns carried by each merchantman.

Norwegian and Danish ships at Manchester after the German invasion of their countries, April 1940.

▲ When launched in 1904, the Firefly was the world's most powerful fire-fighting tug. Her costs were shared between the Manchester Ship Canal Co. and Manchester Fire Brigade, the latter picking up ⅔rds of the bill. In 1924, she was handed over to the Ship Canal Co. so that she could operate in areas outside the fire brigade's jurisdiction.

No.9 Dock taken from No.2 Grain Elevator ▼

179

MANCHESTER SHIP CANAL

In the 1980's, Manchester Docks appear all but derelict yet during the war it played a vital role. The Manchester Ship Canal was considered important enough to be named by Göring as a prime target, when in November 1940, he issued a new directive to the Luftwaffe to commence "economic war" against Britain.

Along with the Thames, Mersey and Bristol Channel, the Ship Canal was to be attacked by minelaying aircraft as well as bombers.

Manchester and Salford docks were important centres for the import of grain and general cargo, but added to these were increasing loads of American and Canadian built military equipment during the build-up to D-Day.

Among the exports from the docks were a number of mobile power stations built by Metrovik for the Soviet Union. Associated with the docks was a gantry, several hundred yards long, built to allow the direct loading of 'Pluto' pipeline in a continuous length from Glover & Co. to vessels moored at Trafford Wharf.

Pics 180/181 show members of the Dock Police taking part in a firefighting exercise. Firefighting was part of their normal duties, though the fire brigade would assist if necessary.

Some of the vast amounts of D-Day equipment that passed through Manchester Docks.

No.9 Dock looking towards No.2 Grain Elevator.

Trafford Wharf looking towards the Swing bridge. The derelict land in the forground is where No.1 Grain Elevator stood. The elevator was destroyed by incendiaries and it is said that the debris smouldered for six months.

VICTORY SPECIAL

Manchester Evening News

23,701 MONDAY, MAY 7, 1945 Three Halfpence

END OF WAR IN EUROPE

Enemy Foreign Minister's Announcement

DOENITZ ORDER: "ALL GERMANS SURRENDER"

"**UNCONDITIONAL surrender of all German fighting troops was ordered by Admiral Doenitz to-day, it was announced by the German Foreign Minister this afternoon.**

THIS ANNOUNCEMENT MEANT THAT A COMPLETE GERMAN SURRENDER HAD BROUGHT THE WAR IN EUROPE TO AN END.

Count von Krosigk said: "German men and women, the High Command of the Armed Forces has to-day, at the order of Grand-Admiral Doenitz, declared the unconditional surrender of all fighting German troops.

"As the leading Minister of the Reich Government, whom the Admiral of the Fleet has appointed for dealing with the war tasks, I turn at this tragic moment of our history of the German nation. After a heroic fight of almost six years of incomparable hardness Germany has succumbed to the overwhelming power of her enemies.

"To continue the war would only mean senseless bloodshed and a futile disintegration. A Government which has a feeling of responsibility for the future of its nation was compelled to act on the collapse of all physical and material forces, and to demand of the enemy the cessation of hostilities.

The broadcast by Krosigk was preceded by a Danish radio flash that all the German forces in Norway—numbering 300,000—had surrendered.

The people of this country learned the news first by Stop Press announcements in the evening papers, then by a B.B.C. announcement at 3 p.m.

All preparations had been made to-day for Mr. Churchill to announce the German surrender from No. 10, Downing-street.

It has been necessary to arrange the simultaneous announcement in all the Allied capitals, but the first flash of victory was all that was necessary to enable the Premier to release the news.

Balcony Hope

The arrival of Ministers in Downing-street was eagerly watched. Telephone calls between Whitehall, Washington, and Moscow were going on, as they have been at frequent intervals for some time.

It was generally hoped that Mr. Churchill would at the end of this announcement address the crowd from the balcony at No. 10.

It was known that announcement by Mr. Churchill this afternoon or this evening would be followed by a broadcast by the King at nine o'clock.

Mr. Churchill's full-scale broadcast will come on Thursday, May 10, the fifth anniversary of his appointment as Prime Minister.

Mr. Churchill will also announce the end of the European War in the Commons, but he will make no lengthy speech. After party leaders have added their few words the Speaker will lead M.P.s to St. Margaret's, Westminster, for a service of thanksgiving. Privy Councillors, Ministers, and M.P.s will follow the Speaker in that order.

On the following day Parliament will not sit.

Doenitz Calls Off the U-boats

THE U-boat war by which the Germans had hoped to starve Britain into submission is ended. Admiral Doenitz, Hitler's successor as Fuhrer, has ordered all German submarines to cease activity, it was reported by the German Flensburg radio to-day. The cease-fire order to the U-boat commanders was given in an Order of the Day on Saturday, added the radio.

Doenitz's order said: "My U-boat men, six years of U-boat warfare lie behind us. You have fought like lions. A crushing superiority has compressed us into a very narrow area. The continuation of the struggle is impossible from the bases which remain.

"U-boat men, unbroken in your warlike courage, you are laying down your arms after a heroic fight which knows no equal. In reverent memory we think of our comrades who have sealed their loyalty to the Fuhrer and Fatherland with their death.

"Comrades, maintain in the future your U-boat spirit with which you have fought at sea, bravely and unflinchingly, during the long years for the welfare of our Fatherland."

It was signed "Your Grand Admiral."

Reuter and A.P.

Frames for First Six New Houses

By a Staff Reporter

STEEL frames for six Phoenix houses, the first to be received in Manchester, were delivered to-day to the Barrow Hill Road site, Cheetham. They are being erected by Taylor Woodrow's, of Bolton, as contractors on behalf of the Ministry of Works.

The delivery date of materials such as asbestos and the kitchen-bathroom units will decide when they will be completed, said a Ministry of Works official to-day.

Some For Salford

Sites have been prepared for 50 of these one-storey temporary asbestos-clad houses by Manchester Corporation. After Ministry of Health approval was secured the roads and sewers were laid for 28 houses in Barrow Hil lRoad, 18 in Northfield Road, Moston, and four in Fairbourne Road, Levenshulme.

The concrete slab base has been laid by the Ministry of Works, who are responsible for building the houses before handing them over to the local authority. They have another contract with the Demolition and Construction Company to erect Phœnix houses in Salford. The Ministry of Works will probably also put up the expected American wooden houses.

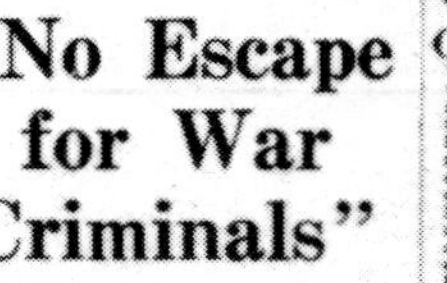

"No Escape for War Criminals"

THERE will be no escape for the German war criminals, said Moscow radio to-day.

"The Russians will grant no amnesty to those who murdered three-year-old Russian children. We shall hold the Germans responsible for the rebuilding of the devastation which they wrought in Russia.

"The Soviet Union and the Allied Nations have no intention of touching the German civil population."—Reuter.

British Push South From Rangoon

British troops, leaving units to mop-up in Rangoon, are pushing south from the city in heavy pre-monsoon rains.

In the oil regions Yenanama, 27 miles south of Minbu, has fallen.—Reuter.

"Lord Haw-Haw" *Not* in Dublin

Reports that "Lord Haw-Haw" was one of the occupants of the German plane which landed at Gormanstown, near Dublin, on Saturday, are untrue.

No News Of King Leopold

Government officials in Brussels said to-day that they had no further news concerning King Leopold.

Court circles have received these tidings with some disquietude.

MUSIC TUTOR DIES

Mrs. Eva Anne Hayes, known as a music teacher in Openshaw as Madame Eva Oldham, has died at her home in Victoria Terrace, Higher Openshaw, aged 47.

TO-DAY'S SHAEF COMMUNIQUE

OUR forces liberated Pilsen, reached the vicinity of Miaersgrun and entered Wesenau, north-west of Pilsen. To the west and south our units reached Tschernoschin and Bischofteinitz and freed Stribro and Klattau. Our infantry reached Kaukowitz and Gutwasser. Other elements reached the Otava River, 20 miles north-east of Regen. South-east of Pilsen we occupied Winterberg and crossed the Muldau River to reach Schattawa. In the area 22 miles north of Linz our units advanced to the Muldau River. South and east of Linz we reached Leonding and Enns. Other elements advanced to Waldneukirchen, south-east of Linz. In the vicinityof Rotpham, 2,000 Hungarians surrendered to our forces.

"GOEBBELS' BODY FOUND IN BERLIN"

GOEBBELS'S body and those of his family have been found in an air-raid shelter near the Berlin Reichstag, according to unconfirmed reports reaching Moscow.

Many explanations have been offered to account for the disappearance of Goebbels. One of the latest, which fits in with the report of the finding of his body, is that he perished in a suicide pact with his wife and his entire family.

There is still no trace of Hitler. Special Soviet investigators are questioning captured Nazis in an attempt to reconstruct events leading up to his disappearance.—Reuter.

STRAITS: Blaze of sunshine and quickly mounting temperature.

Light W.-S.-W. breeze just rippled the sea.

TATTOO

Germans Told "No Beer"

SALE of alcoholic drinks of every kind, including strong beer, has been prohibited in Wilhelmshaven by the Allied authorities. According to Wilhelmshaven radio all inns not serving meals are to be closed. A curfew has been imposed and "unnecessary standing about in the streets" is forbidden.—Reuter.

THE POLICE STAND BY—JUST IN CASE

METROPOLITAN policemen were standing by to-day, in readiness for the expected announcement that the war had ended, to deal with the crowds of revellers expected to converge in the West End.

Service police of all the Allies were also ready for their patrols.

The civil police pool consisted of hundreds of men who can be rushed to any spot where the situation might show signs of getting out of hand.

The police will take drastic action against revellers only if they attempt to damage public or private property, and will look with a fatherly eye on anyone who celebrates too much. Only if a person is incapable or unruly will he be taken into "protective custody."

No special arrangements have been made for controlling the crowds in Manchester I was told at police headquarters to-day.

"We are always able to call out more police in an emergency," said an official.

The people celebrate.

191

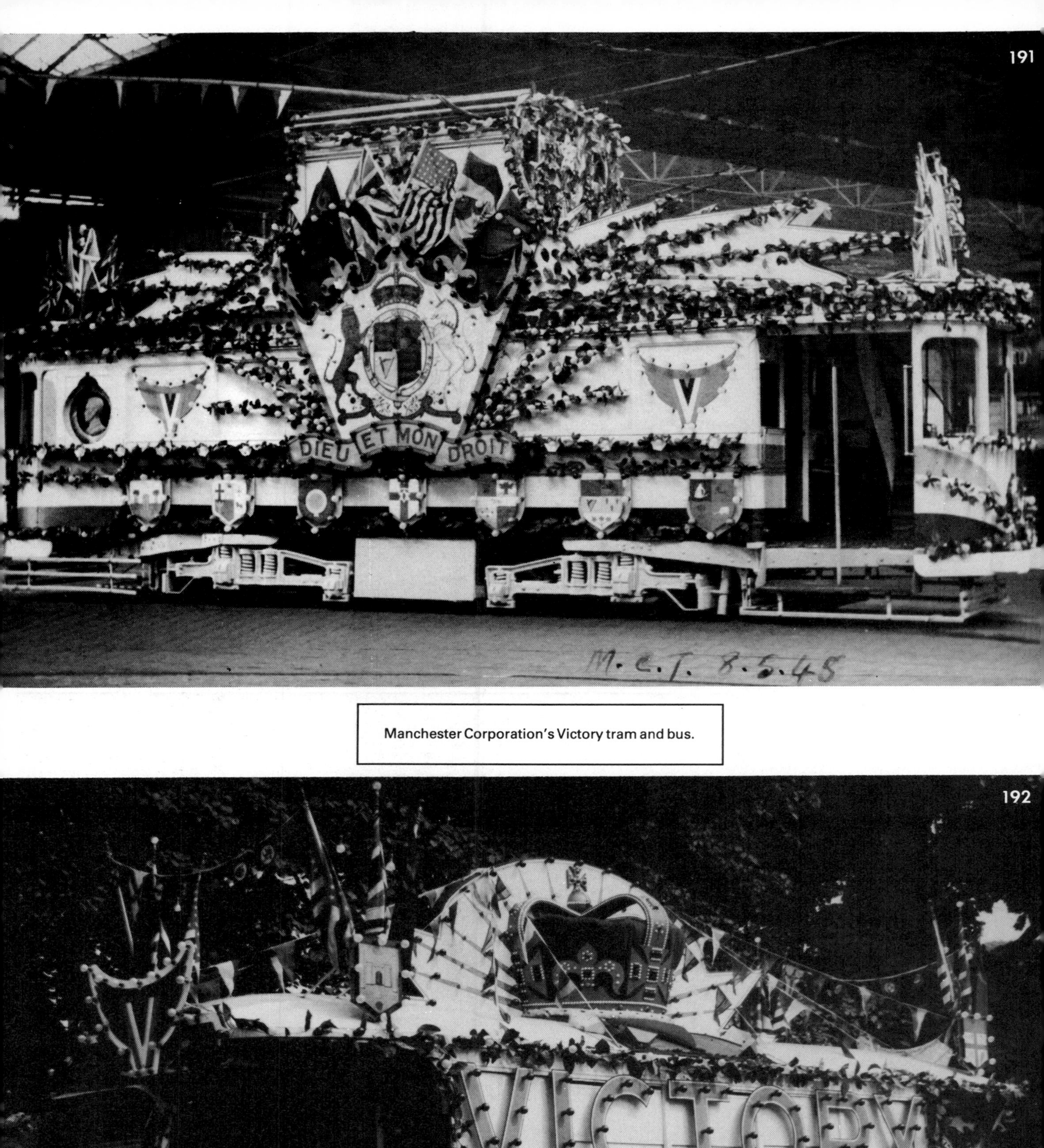

Manchester Corporation's Victory tram and bus.

192

194

Victory celebrations at Ferranti's, Moston.

195

196

197

CITY EDITION B

Manchester Evening News

23,785 TUESDAY, AUGUST 14, 1945 Three Halfpence

'JAPAN ACCEPTS' —SWISS RADIO

MANY HOURS WAIT FOR LONG CODED NOTE

Swiss radio announced this afternoon that Japan had accepted the Allied terms.

Swiss radio said: "Japanese Information Office reported the acceptance of the Allied capitulation formula, on the basis of a statement by the Japanese War Ministry.

U.S. radio monitors reported shortly before noon to-day: "Japanese radio has begun to get in touch with all Japanese ships at sea."

TOKYO radio put out a Japanese News Agency statement to-day that an Imperial message "accepting the Potsdam ultimatum" would be forthcoming shortly. While no elaboration of this message was available, it was assumed at U.S. headquarters at Guam that it meant acceptance of both the Potsdam terms and the U.S. Note making further conditions outlining the subservience of the Japanese Emperor to the Allied Commander-in-Chief.

Domei Agency messages said that a full statement of the reply—which the agency apparently assumed to mean complete surrender—would be available between 1 p.m. and 2 p.m. to-day.

From New York Federal Communications Commission engineers reported that Tokyo code station had been sending long code messages to Switzerland since 5 48 a.m. to-day. It was added that two Japanese transmitters "signed off" at 8 28 (British Summer Time).

A Berne message via Paris said that the Tokyo message, which was very long, was being deciphered, and would be handed to the U.S. and Chinese Embassies "this afternoon."

If the Japanese reply does, in fact, accept all the Allied terms laid down by the Big Four, it will presumably be followed by the Allied proclamations bringing the Pacific War to an end.

Fleet Cheers

It was stated in Washington that no White House announcement was expected before 2 p.m. (British Time). It was pointed out that normal transmission time of a Note sent through a neutral Power was 12 hours.

President Truman's naval aide arrived at the White House at 2 a.m. (7 a.m. B.S.T.), and other officials were expected to assemble there.

The U.S. Fleet H.Q. communications room at Guam Island flashed over Guam radio to-day that Tokyo radio had reported acceptance of the Allied

★ Turn to Back Page Col. 1

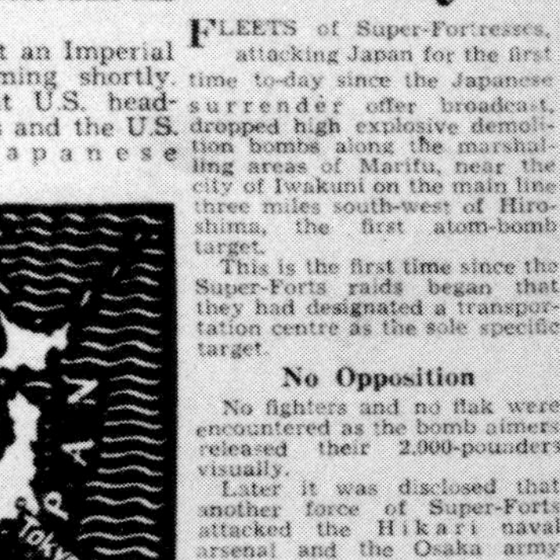

Potsdam's Points

MAIN points from the 13-point Potsdam declaration of July 26, issued by the United States, Britain, and China, which called for the unconditional surrender of all Japan's armed forces, were:

"There must be eliminated for all time the authority and influence of those who have deceived and misled the people of Japan into embarking on world conquest, for we insist that a new order of peace, security, and justice will be impossible unless irresponsible militarism is driven from the world;

"Until such a new order is established, and until there is convincing proof that Japan's war-making power is destroyed, points in Japanese territory designated by the Allies shall be occupied:

"Japanese sovereignty shall be limited to the islands of Honshu, Hokkaido, Kyushu, Shikoku, and such minor islands as we determine:

"Japanese military forces to be completely disarmed and sent home:

"Japanese war industries to be destroyed and reparations exacted in kind."—Reuter.

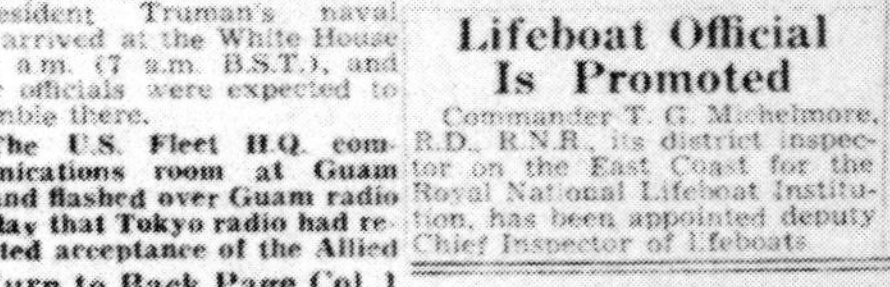

BUT THERE ARE FRESH TERMS ABOUT EMPEROR

JAPANESE NEWS AGENCY statements on the surrender offer refer only to the Potsdam Declaration and not to the terms sent to the Japanese Government through Switzerland on Saturday afternoon, in reply to the Japanese offer to accept the Potsdam terms on condition that the Emperor is allowed to remain. These terms were:

1. The Japanese Emperor and Government are to subject their authority to that of an Allied Supreme Commander. General MacArthur has been unofficially mentioned for the post;
2. The Emperor is to order the surrender of Japanese troops in all theatres;
3. The Japanese Government is to transport prisoners and civilian internees to places of safety immediately;
4. The Japanese people are to be free to decide their ultimate form of government;
5. Allied troops are to remain in Japan for a specified period. —Reuter.

CLOSING V J DAYS

On the V(J) Days, the Baltic Exchange will close.

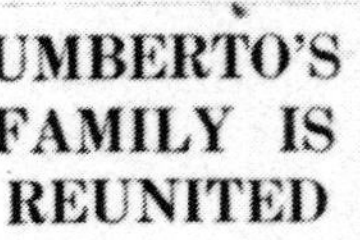

UMBERTO'S FAMILY IS REUNITED

CHOKING with emotion, a Crown Prince stood on an airfield, to-day, and saw his wife and children—taken from him by the war—for the first time in two years.

He is Prince Umberto, Lieut.-General of the Italian Realm, who resumed normal domestic life to-day at Quirinale Palace in Italy.

B.U.P.

Leave Train Casualties May be Very Big

THIRTY-SIX hours after the big B.L.A. leave train crash in darkness early yesterday morning, a mile east of Goch, it was still impossible to obtain a definite casualty list to-day.

The total dead and injured list, it is feared, is very heavy. The train from Brussels, proceeding to Munster, crashed head-on on a single line with a westbound leave train from Germany heading for Nijmegen.

Both trains were crammed with troops standing and lying in the coaches.

Eye-witnesses say the eastbound train was travelling about 10 miles an hour and the other between 35 and 40.

Locos Interlocked

The locomotives crashed together with great impact and became interlocked. The first two carriages of the eastbound train were thrown violently from the line and troops travelling in that, including Canadians, said there were many casualties in both coaches.

The first coach of the westbound train mounted the tender locomotive and was badly smashed. About a dozen are believed dead in this coach.

The second coach of this train was also damaged.

Troops say that crowding was increased in the Munster-bound train by the fact that three coaches were taken off at Nijmegen immediately before the crash and soldiers from these coaches crammed into the remainder.—B.U.P.

Petain May Know To-night

PHILIPPE PETAIN, Marshal of France, may know his fate to-night when 24 jurors are expected to decide whether or not he is guilty of plotting against the Republic and of "intelligence with the enemy."

Petain will not ask for mercy should he be sentenced to death, said his counsel, M. Fernand Payen, in a dramatic speech yesterday. "There is his head. Take it if you wish," said M. Payen.

Under French law, however, any one in France can file a petition for mercy on Petain's behalf even if Petain himself disdains to do so.

De Gaulle's Right

In any case, General de Gaulle, as head of the State, would have the traditional right to commute, if he thinks fit, the death sentence, should it be passed.

There was a heated scene in the court last night when the jurors' request for an adjournment raised doubts about the trial finishing to-day.

M. Isorni, Petain's defence counsel, said the defence could finish its case by 7 p.m. Then the judge will question the jury before they retire.

Want To Relax

Whether the trial lasts into Wednesday morning depends on how long the jury deliberate, but they are determined to reach a verdict before rising so they can relax to-morrow, a bank holiday.

Paris Press May Stop

PARIS may be without newspapers to-night. The French Press Federation yesterday announced that two evening papers, "Liberation" and "Soir Libres," have run out of newsprint.

Both papers are invoking an agreement whereby all Paris newspapers pledged themselves to cease publication if one or more found themselves unable to carry on because of shortage of newsprint.

The French Ministry for Production and the Ministry of Information say the newspapers were repeatedly warned they must not exceed their quota by reverting to pre-war sizes during the Petain trial.—B.U.P.

Army Helps Jews To Return Home

Two hundred German and Austrian Jews, who sought refuge in Belgium have returned to their homes with the aid of the British military authorities.

Their return is contrary to the recommendation of the World Jewish Congress, but Jewish organisations in Belgium did not oppose it because of the impoverished conditions in Belgium.

Town's Grand-Scale Plans For V J Day

Worsley, whose area includes Walkden, Boothstown, and Little Hulton, have appointed a special committee to make all arrangements for a mammoth V J celebration — the greatest celebration in the town's history. Events will centre around the Parr Fold Park and a huge bonfire is being assembled which will be lit at midnight on the day on which victory is declared irrespective of the hour.

Gardeners To Hold Shows Next Year

Members of the Heywood and District Horticultural Society have decided to hold shows as usual next year.

The Mayor, Councillor W. Taylor, has been elected president, Councillor F. Brown chairman of the committee, Mr. G. J. Griffiths secretary, and Mr. F. Schofield treasurer.

DE GAULLE'S U.S. TRIP

General de Gaulle will arrive in Washington on August 22 to confer with President Truman, says a Paris message.—B.U.P.

Demolition Bombs On Railways

FLEETS of Super-Fortresses, attacking Japan for the first time to-day since the Japanese surrender offer broadcast, dropped high explosive demolition bombs along the marshalling areas of Marifu, near the city of Iwakuni on the main line three miles south-west of Hiroshima, the first atom-bomb target.

This is the first time since the Super-Forts raids began that they had designated a transportation centre as the sole specific target.

No Opposition

No fighters and no flak were encountered as the bomb aimers released their 2,000-pounders visually.

Later it was disclosed that another force of Super-Forts attacked the Hikari naval arsenal and the Osaka army arsenal.

As a force of over 1,000 British and American carrier planes from Admiral William Halsey's U.S. Third Fleet struck at six airfields protecting Tokyo's metropolitan area yesterday, U.S. warships nearly 1,100 miles away were bombarding three military positions in the Kuriles, Japan's northerly outposts.

Naval Attack

The U.S. naval force split up into three attack groups to deliver simultaneous bombardments on two points in Paramushiro in the extreme north of the Kuriles, and Matua Island, 110 miles to the south.

Attacking in broad daylight some of the units went so close inshore that the Japanese replied with machine-gun fire. Going in the warships sank 10 Japanese trawlers and a submarine chaser.

The previous day over 600 land-based bombers and fighters—the biggest air fleet ever sent

† Turn to Back Page Col. 6

Lifeboat Official Is Promoted

Commander T. G. Michelmore, R.D., R.N.R., its district inspector on the East Coast for the Royal National Lifeboat Institution, has been appointed deputy Chief Inspector of Lifeboats

LAST EDITION EXTRA B

Manchester Evening News

23,782 FRIDAY, AUGUST 10, 1945 Three Halfpence

THE JAPANESE SURRENDER

One Condition—That Emperor Remains

"WE ACCEPT THE POTSDAM ULTIMATUM," SAYS TOKYO

JAPAN surrendered to the Allies to-day on one condition. She accepted the Potsdam Ultimatum, stipulating only that the Emperor's position as Sovereign Ruler should be safeguarded.

At 12 42 this afternoon a dramatic flash announced that the Tokyo Government had asked the Swiss and Swedish Governments to transmit a communication to Britain, the U.S.A., Russia, and China.

Immediately afterwards Tokyo Radio announced the Japanese decision in the following terms:

"The Japanese Government is ready to accept the terms of the joint declaration which was issued at Potsdam by the heads of the Governments of the United States, Britain, China, and later subscribed to by the Soviet Government. Acceptance is made with the understanding that the declaration does not comprise any demand which prejudices the prerogatives of His Majesty as Emperor."

The Potsdam ultimatum invited the Japanese to surrender on the terms that the authority of the present Japanese Government should be ended; that points on Japanese territory should be occupied; that Japanese sovereignty should be limited to the main islands of Japan and such minor islands as the Allies should decide; that Japan should be completely disarmed and all war industries destroyed; and that free speech, religion and thought should be permitted.

The Japanese announcement came after Japanese radio listeners had been warned to stand by for "a sensational message which the people of the war-torn world have been waiting for and longing to hear."

Afer Tokyo radio had broadcast this Japanese News Agency message to the world, the announcer said: "The Japanese Government hopes sincerely . . . ." At this point the transmission was interrupted. There was a further service warning of "Stand By," but the news agency then went off the air.

The Russian Advance

Immediately on receipt of the news of the Tokyo broadcast President Truman called a U.S. Cabinet meeting in Washington.

It was stated in Washingto nto-day that some days might elapse before a decision could be come to, but official circles believe strongly that the Allies will be willing to accept the Emperor as a "puppet" who took no direct part beyond submission to the War Lords' plans. His presence, it is felt, would not be incompatible with the rejuvenation of Japan as a democratic State.

This afternoon the Japanese offer had not reached London. After it is received there may be a lengthy exchange of views between London, Washington, Moscow, and Chungking.

When the Tokyo decision was made known to-day hte Russian armies were pouring across Manchuria after smashing through the Japanese defences.

Russian forces had also invaded Korea, in the vicinity of Keiko, and in the island of Sakhalin, the southern half, ceded to Japan by the Russians after 1904-5 war, had been inavded by Russian troops after a bombardment.

Russian Cossacks were reported to-day to be following up the armour and mopping-up, while a great weight of infantry was nullifying all Japanese counter-attacks.—Reuter, A.P., and B.U.P.

"GOD-SENT RULER"

THE following is an extract from an article by O. M. Green, which appeared in the "Manchester Evening News" on May 18:—

Now just 44, he has five daughters and two sons and is described as a model father and husband who has never allowed his thoughts to stray among the lovelies of his court.

He is abstemious and frugal. For recreation he is fond of botany and marine biology.

But it is as Emperor not man that Hirohito has been considered, a god to be worshipped, a high priest to lead the sacrifices in the animal festivals.

Theoretically omnipotent, in practice with no more power than his Government permits. Hirohito came to the throne in 1926 when a wave of real Liberalism was flowing through Japan.

It is said that he had ideas of becoming a genuinely constitutional monarch.

Hirohito was at first seen in public more frequently than his predecessor, but in 1931 the Army knocked his Liberal ideas on the head.

Hirohito's outings were stopped and now he travels behind shuttered windows. As he drives through the streets no one may look from an upper window as that would mean looking down on the Emperor.

Japan deeply venerates the "God-sent ruler of the great Japanese Empire.

How Japan Gave News

HERE is the full text of the Tokyo "surrender" broadcast to-day:

"By gracious command of His Majesty, the Emperor, who, to enhance the cause of world peace, desires earnestly to bring about an early termination of hostilites with a view to saving mankind from calamities which would be imposed upon them by further continuation of war.

"The Japanese Government to-day addressed the following communication to the Swiss and Swedish Governments respectively, for transmission to the United States, Great Britain, China and the Soviet Union.

"The Japanese is ready to accept terms of the joint declaration issued at Potsdam, July 26, 1945, by the heads of the governments of United States, Britain and China, and later subscribed to by the Soviet Union, with the understanding that the said declaration does not compromise any demand which prejudices the prerogatives of His Majesty as sovereign ruler.

"The Japanese Government hopes sincerely that this . . ."

Here the Japanese radio went off the air saying, "stand by."—B.U.P.

8,000 Will be Freed

By a Staff Reporter

PEACE in the Pacific will be Welcomed with thanksgiving in at least 8,000 Lancashire and Cheshire homes, for that is the number of men from the two counties who are posted as prisoners of war in the hands of the Japanese.

Flash That Told "The End"

```
FCW .   BUP FLASH - 12.42
JAPANESE ACCEPT POTSDAM ULTIMATUM .
END FLASH
```

Crowds in City Cheer the End

By a Staff Reporter

NEWS of Japan's collapse came when tens of thousands of city workers were at lunch. A few minutes after 10 past one the *Manchester Evening News* came out with an edition, containing the Stop Press announcement that Japan had accepted the ultimatum and newsvendors calling "Special" were quickly surrounded by the crowds.

Within a few minutes one newspaper seller sold five dozen papers and another, unable to cope with the eager buyers, put his cap on the pavement, spread his papers nearby and invited the people to help themselves. They did.

Hold-up

The news spread quickly, and groups of people reading over one another's shoulders raised a cheer which was taken up by others in Cross-street and Albert Square as well as in many of the packed restaurants.

A number of lorries laden with fish were passing down Cross-street, and the first driver pulled up to buy a paper. Others followed suit, and soon there was a long line of waiting vehicles.

Until someone shouted the good news to him, the policeman on traffic duty must have thought there had been an accident, for he was on his way to investigate the hold-up.

Flags of the United Nations were soon run up, and in Piccadilly young workers danced and sang as the last enemy fell.

Outside the American Red Cross, in King-street, a U.S. sergeant pulled himself to attention and mumbled several times "Well, I'll be doggoned."

SALAZAR SEES ENVOY

Dr. Salazar, the Portuguese Premier, received the new British ambassador, Sir Owen O'Malley.

The World is at Peace

By George Campey

IT began and it has ended with the Japanese. Fourteen years ago the ambitious leaders of Japan set their armies marching into Manchuria and thereby shook the foundations of world peace.

It became a world of uncertainty, of fear. The cue was given to the dictators. They armed, they prepared — and then, following the Japanese example, they marched.

In October, 1935, Britain and the rest of the world had a shock when Mussolini's young Fascists went into Abyssinia with their tanks, flame-throwers and planes to oppose the spears and rifles of the natives.

Then Hitler

That war came to an end. For a moment the world breathed relief—but an uncertain relief. Then on Good Friday, 1939, Mussolini struck again — this time at Albania.

The dictators were setting the pace. Hitler, no less than Mussolini, was becoming ambitious.

His entry into Austria had not satisfied him, nor the demands of Czecho-Slovakia. Mr. Chamberlain's famous journey to meet Hitler was in vain.

The air was full of threats and appeasement. Nobody wanted war, but what was the answer to the dictators? In September, 1939, the answer came.

September, 1939

On September 1 Germany invaded Poland, and two days later Britain and France were

★ Turn to Back Page Col. 3

Terms of the Potsdam Ultimatum.—Back Page.

Waving their Victory Editions the crowds outside the "Manchester Evening News" building went wild with excitement.

▲ VE celebrations at Crumpsall Lane School.

202

▲ VJ Party, Richmond Street, Moss Side.

A group of ex-P.O.W's visit the crank-grinding section at Manchester Corporation Transport's Hyde Road Works. ▼

203

"FACT FILE"

1939

1.9.39 Evacuation of Manchester's schoolchildren begins.
Germany invades Poland.
Italy proclaims non-belligerent status.
Norway, Switzerland and Finland declare their neutrality.

2.9.39 Eire declares her neutrality.

3.9.39 Last day of evacuations.
Britain and France declare war on Germany.
India, Australia and New Zealand declare war on Germany.
Belgium declares her neutrality.
"SS Athenia" torpedoed and sunk without a warning by a U-Boat in contradiction of Hitler's order.
Nationwide air-raid warning.

4.9.39 Advance units of B.E.F. land in France.

10.9.39 Canada delares war on Germany.

17.9.39 Soviet Russia invades Poland.

27.9.39 Poland surrenders.
Sir John Simon introduces our first Emergency War Budget.

29.9.39 Russia and Germany formally divide Poland.

6.10.39 Hitler offers peace settlement to Britain and France.

11.10.39 BEF strength stands at 158,000 men.

12.10.39 Hitler's peace proposals rejected.

14.10.39 HMS 'Royal Oak' sunk in Scapa Flow.

8.11.39 Assassination attempt on Hitler fails.

30.11.39 Russia invades Finland.

3.12.39 Conscription in Britain extended to all males aged 19-41. Females aged 20-30 required to work as auxiliaries or on defence jobs.

29.12.39 Finns defeat Russians at Suommusalmi

1940

5.1.40 Hore-Belisha sacked as Minister of War.

8.1.40 Rationing of basic food stuffs introduced in Britain.
Finns defeat Russians at Karelian.

27.1.40 Winston Churchill spoke in public at Manchester; his theme being the expansion of jobs for the war effort.
(There were still over 1 million unemployed.)

11.2.40 Russians launch massive attacks against Finland.

17.2.40 400,000 more children evacuated from British cities.

12.3.40 Russian-Finish war ends.

29.3.40 Russia declares her neutrality in the European war.

10.5.40 Germany invades the Low Countries.

13.5.40 Germany invades France. Liege falls.

18.5.40 Antwerp falls to Germans.

26.5.40 Evacuation of allied troops from Dunkirk begins.

9.6.40 Norway stops fighting.

10.6.40 Neville Chamberlain resigns as Prime Minister and is succeeded by Winston Churchill.

14.6.40 Anthony Eden appeals for men to join the Local Defence Volunteers.

17.6.40 France sues for peace.

18.6.40 Italy declares war on France and Britain.

20.6.40 0134 hrs. First serious air-raid alert in Manchester.
ARP and Civil Defence posts fully manned.

30.6.40 Guernsey occupied by German forces.

2.7.40 Hitler issues orders for the invasion of Britain.

19.7.40 Hitler offers peace terms to Britain.

29.7.40 Stray German bomber drops a bomb in the Salford area.

8.8.40 First air attack in Manchester area. Over Salford, a German bomber dropped a bundle of leaflets which failed to open and fell on the head of a police officer guarding the entrance to the Civil Defence Report and Control Centre.

15.8.40 Luftwaffe launch all-out assault in an attempt to cripple RAF.

28/9.8.40 HE on Baguley, Brooklands and Worsley. Casualties at Altrincham.

29/30.8.40 HE on Hulme. Incendiaries drop on Moss Side, Alexandra Park, Rusholme and Platt Fields.

30/31.8.40. Pendlebury and Swinton attacked with HE.

31/1.9.40 Lone raider drops HE damaging Palace Theatre. Rumour spreads that many people were killed.

3/4.9.40 Chorlton-cum-Hardy bombed.

4/5.9.40 HE dropped on Weaste Cemetary. Oil storage depot hit. Old peoples home at Hope Hospital damaged. Other bombs fall on Pendleton.

6/7.9.40 Worsley bombed.

7.9.40 London Blitz begins.

8/9.9.40. Didsbury and Northernden hit - no casualties.

16.9.40. USA introduces conscription.
Bombs drop on Heaton Park.

24/5.9.40. Vichy French planes bomb Gibralter.

25/6.9.40. Worsley hit again. HE bombs kill 32 sheep. HE also falls on Sale and Swinton. Stretford attacked with incendiaries.

1/2.10.40. HE/incendiary raid over Platt Fields, Moss Side, Fallowfield and Withington. Three killed and three injured. Houses in Lower Kersal area of Salford damaged.

2/3.10.40. Railway yard at Princes Bridge, Water Street hit by HE. Newton Heath, Moston and Parrswood also hit. Oil bombs land on Salford goods station, which being full of bales of cotton waste is gutted by fire. HE bomb lands in the grounds of Lancaster House and another crashes through the roof of Salford Town Hall.

3.10.40. Neville Chamberlain, now a very sick man, resigns from the Government.

7/8.10.40. Collyhurst and Hulme attacked. Incendiaries drop on Trafford Park and Stretford.

9.10.40. Incendiary attacks on Chorlton-cum-Hardy, Moss Side and Chorltun-on-Medlock. HE bombs land on Swinton, Eccles, Urmston, Worsley and Trafford Park.

10/11.10.40. Three alerts. Incendiary attack on Salford. HE on Disbury. Northernden, Chorlton, Hulme and Old Trafford.

11/12.10.40. Moss Side, Hulme, Chorlton-on-Medlock, Rusholme, Fallowfield, Didsbury bombed. A heavy bomb penetrated two floors of the nurses home at the Manchester Royal Infirmary before exploding - miraculously no-one was hurt.

18/19.10.40. Sale bombed.

26.10.40. Didsbury bombed.

28.10.40. Italy invades Greece.
8.11.40. Italians suffer major defeat by the Greeks.
9.11.40. Chamberlain dies.
14/15.11.40. Coventry devastated in an eleven hour attack.
18.11.40. Wythenshaw and Stretford attacked.
29/30.11.40. Many buildings in Altrincham damaged by bomb blast.
16.12.40. Short sharp raid on Ancoats district.
23.12.40. London Fire Brigade send reinforcements to help Manchester.

1941

1/2.1.41 Gorton area attacked. Heavy bomb scores a direct hit on a surface shelter at Withington - 9 killed.
9/10.1.41 Widespread incendiary raid on city.
21.1.41 "Daily Worker" closed down under the Defence Regulations.
21.1.41 Tobruk falls to British and Australian troops.
12.2.41 German troops land at Tripoli.
13.2.41 King George VI and Queen Elizabeth visit Manchester.
11.3.41 3 hour raid over several districts. Stretford, Trafford Park and Pamona Docks hit. £50,000 worth of damage caused to Manchester United's ground when bomb drops on the centre stand. The dressing rooms are burnt out and the medical room is destroyed.
5.4.41 German troops invade Greece.
15.4.41 Salford bombed.
18.4.41 British War Relief Society of USA visit Manchester.
20.4.41 Greeks surrender.
1.5.41 Chorlton-cum-Hardy bombed.
2/3.5.41 HE bombs dropped on Sretford. 4 killed, 4 injured.
7/8.5.41 Widespread but relatively light air raid. Anti-aircraft batteries bring down a raider which crashes onto Torkington Golf Course.
10.5.41 Rudolf Hess lands in Scotland.
20.5.41 Major anti-gas exercise held by Manchester's ARP in Piccadilly.
1/2.6.41 Manchester's third heaviest raid of the war.
22.6.41 Germany invades Russia on a 1,800 mile front with 3 million troops, 3,580 tanks, 1,830 warplanes and 600,000 vehicles. Clothes rationing introduced.
18.8.41 National Fire Service comes into being.
2.9.41 German troops within 20 miles of Leningrad.
11.9.41 A squadron of tanks pay an official visit to Manchester, going on show in Albert Square.
22.9.41 "Tank for Russia" week begins in British arms factories.
25.10.41. Altrincham bombed.
1.12.41 German armoured units within 9 miles of the Kremlin.
7.12.41 Japanese carrier-based planes attack the US Pacific Fleet at Pearl Harbour.
8.12.41 Britain and America declar war on the Empire of Japan.
11.12.41 America declares war on Germany and Italy.

1942

15.2.42. Singapore falls to the Japanese.
4/8.5.42. Battle of Coral Sea.
6.5.42. Corregidor falls to Japanese.
4/6.6.42. Battle of Midway.
21.6.42. Tobruk falls to Rommel.
27.7.42. Lone raider drops stick of bombs on Beswick. 3 killed.
13.8.42. HMS Manchester sunk off Tunisia.
19.8.42. Canadian and British raiding forces land at Dieppe.
25.8.42. HRH Duke Kent killed in plane crash.
20.9.42. Battle for Stalingrad.
4.11.42. Afrika Korps defeated at El Alamein.

1943.

2.2.43. German 6th Army surrenders at Stalingrad.
13.3.43. Assassination attempt on Adolph Hitler fails.
20.3.43. Second assassination attempt on Hitler fails.
12.5.43. Surrender of all Axis forces in North Africa.
10.7.43. Allies land in Sicily.
24.7.43. RAF attack Hamburg with 740 planes.
25.7.43. RAF attack Essen with 627 planes.
27.7.43. RAF attack Dresden with 739 planes. 20,000 men, women and children are thought to have died in the firestorms created by incendiary bombs.
8.9.43. Italian surrender made public, though a secret armistice had been signed on the 3rd.
13.10.43. Italy declares war on Germany.

1944

14.1.44. Education Act passed.
22.1.44. Allies land at Anzio.
6.6.44. D-Day landings in Normandy.
22.6.44. Russia launches her summer offensive on a 300 mile front.
24.7.44. "Hitler salutes" made the mandatory form of salute in the German Army.
25.8.44. Liberation of Paris.
13.12.44. Home Guard stood down.
24.12.44. V1 attack launched against Manchester. It fails though 27 people are killed when one falls on Oldham.

1945

1.1.45 Lloyd George made a peer.
15.1.45 First boat train to Paris since 1940 leaves London Victoria.
7.3.45 US troops cross the Rhine at Remagen.
23.3.45 British troops cross the Rhine.
1.4.45 Cheese ration cut.
12.4.45 Roosevelt dies.
23.4.45 Blackout restrictions lifted.
25.4.45 US and Soviet forces meet at the Elbe.
28.4.45 Mussolini and his mistress are executed by Italian partisans.
29.4.45 German forces in Italy surrender.
30.4.45 Adolf Hitler commits suicide.
1.5.45 Last ARP workers are give a months notice.
4.5.45 German forces in North-West Europe capitulate to Montgomery.
7.5.45 Unconditional surrender of German forces.
8.5.45 Trafford Park was the scene of great confusion. Hundreds of people turned up for work only to be turned away, Many people were under the impression that the VE Day national holiday did not begin until the Prime Ministers broadcast at 3.00 p.m.
By 10.00 a.m. more than 300 people gathered in Albert Sqaure to see the flags of the 44 allied nations go up - but they didn't. A Town Hall official explained that the ceremony would not take place until Churchill's official broadcast to the nation at 3.00 p.m.
22.5.45 Rations cut again.
23.5.45 Churchill resigns and forms a caretaker government.
15.6.45 Parliament dissolved.

5.7.45	General Election.
22.7.45	Tea ration increased to 2½ozs per person per week.
26.7.45	Labour party sweep to power with 393 seats.
6.8.45	Atom bomb dropped in Hiroshima.
9.8.45	Atom bomb dropped on Nagasaki.
12.8.45	Two crowded troop trains involved in head-on crash a mile east of Goch.
14.8.45	Surrender of Japan. Worsley, whose area included Walkden, Boothstown and Little Hulton appointed a special committee to make all arrangements for VJ celebrations. Events were to be centred around Parr Fold Park where a huge bonfire was to be erected to be lit at midnight on the day victory was declared.
1.9.45.	Clothing ration cut by 25%.
19.9.45.	William Joyce (Lord Haw Haw) sentenced to death for treason.
1.10.45.	Restaurant cars restored to trains. (3 course lunch cost 3s 6d).
8.10.45.	Ban on central heating in shops, offices and places of entertainment is lifted.
23.10.45.	Income Tax reduced from 10s to 9s in the pound.
19.11.45.	Government announces plans to nationalise coal, gas and electricity.
22.11.45.	Nuremberg trials begin. Petrol reduced to 1s 11d per gallon.
20.12.45.	Labour controls end. People now free to seek their own jobs.

CAN YOU HELP?

"MANCHESTER AT WAR VOLUME 2"

Volume 2 is currently being researched and we invite you, the reader, to assist us.

Any photographs and stories you may have hidden away of wartime Manchester or indeed any other cities around the country, are of interest to us with a view to possible inclusion in future publications.

If you think you may be able to help please send your material to the address below:-

Research Dept.,
Archive Publications Ltd.,
27 York Road,
Bowdon,
Cheshire.
WA14 3EF.

We regret that we are only able to return material if you enclose the appropriate sized Stamped Addressed Envelope (SAE).

Thanking you in anticipation.

Archive Publications Ltd.

ACKNOWLEDGEMENTS

Chief Constable James Anderton OBE; Birmingham Post & Mail; Birmingham Reference Library; Boat Museum, Ellesmere Port; Station Officer Bonner; British Aerospace Ltd. (Manchester Division); Duncan Brodie; Susan Browning; David Burgess-Wise; George Cogswell; Daily Mirror; Derby Evening Telegraph; Ferranti; Ford Motors; GEC Traction Ltd.; Colonel Gibbs; Greater Manchester Fire Brigade Museum; Greater Manchester Police Force Museum; Greater Manchester Transport Museum; Graeme Hague; Harry Holmes; Pat Huscroft; Imperial War Museum; Peter Lloyd; London Fire Brigade Museum; Dr. Peter McNiven; Fred Mabbott; Manchester Evening News; Manchester Town Hall Planning Dept. and City Engineers;

Manchester University Library; Paul Matthews; Metro Cammell; Suzanne Miles; Stan Nelson; Nuclear Engineering Industries (NEI); Osdall Hall Museum; Dr. Mike Pegg; The Photo Source; John Pollock; Port of Manchester (Manchester Ship Canal); Phil Redeyoff; Anton Rippon; Rolls-Royce Derby; Rolls-Royce Heritage Trust Museum; Rita Rowe; Stan Royal; Salford Local History Library; Doreen Scott; Mike Shaw; Simon Engineering; Southern Evening Echo; Martin Steiger; Trafford Park Estates; Chris Trotter; George Turnbull; Barry Ulyatt; Vickers Specialist Engine Division, Crewe; Cliff Wimpenny; Furness Withy (Manchester Liners).

Please forgive any possible omissions. Every effort has been made to include all organisations and individuals involved in the preparation of this Book.